APPROACHES TO
LITERATURE THROUGH
LITERARY FORM

APPROACHES TO LITERATURE THROUGH LITERARY FORM

THE ORYX READING MOTIVATION SERIES

BY PAULA KAY MONTGOMERY

ORYX PRESS
1995

The rare Arabian Oryx is believed to have inspired the myth of the unicorn. This desert antelope became virtually extinct in the early 1960s. At that time several groups of international conservationists arranged to have 9 animals sent to the Phoenix Zoo to be the nucleus of a captive breeding herd. Today the Oryx population is over 1000 and over 500 have been returned to the Middle East.

Library of Congress Cataloging-in-Publication Data

Montgomery, Paula Kay.
    Approaches to literature through literary form / by Paula Kay Montgomery.
        p. cm.— (The Oryx reading motivation series)
    Includes bibliographical references.
    ISBN 0-89774-775-5 (pbk.)
    1. Literary form—Study and teaching—United States. 2. Literature—Study and
teaching—United States. 3. Reading—United States. 4. Motivation in education—
United States. I. Title. II. Series.
LB1575.5.U5M65 1995
372.64'044—dc20   95-23876
                                                                        CIP

Contents

Series Statement

What makes an individual want to turn the page and read more? That question has puzzled many in the field of education. The answer is not always forthcoming. And, the answer is not the same for every individual. However, that is the question that prompted this series of books about getting students to read. The Oryx Reading Motivation Series focuses on the materials and approaches that seem to be prominent for grouping literature. The prime purpose for the investigation is to identify promising methods, techniques, and strategies that might motivate students or get students in grades five through nine to "turn the page."

Each book in the series examines a particular approach to grouping literature: thematic, subject, genre, literary form, chronological, author, and comprehension skills. In each case, the literature is grouped for presentation in a different way to meet a specific purpose. For example, the comprehension-skills approach groups literature useful for teaching the same skill. That skill might be comparison: literature of all types that might be grouped together to exemplify the pattern of comparison. Literary form examines the structure of the literary work, such as the diary, novel, short story, and so forth, with an emphasis on the elements of those structures, including plot, characterization, etc. An author approach provides a study of the works of one author that might allow students to examine style, growth, and changes a writer has undergone. Works written over a given period of time or at the same time might be grouped for a chronological approach. Such an approach allows the reader to examine interrelationships between writers and their society. The interest of students in a particular subject makes the subject approach useful for grouping different literary formats and forms about the same subject. The genre approach capitalizes on particular student interests or skills, such as problem solving or history, and combines this with works of similar literary form and subject patterns. And, finally, the thematic approach groups materials around a common theme that may be investigated in depth by students.

Each book in the series is written for the classroom teacher and library media specialist. This partnership offers rich possibilities for combining the knowledge of teaching and literary content with the multiple resources of two professions that have long addressed literature and have searched for ways to make students want to turn the pages. Although the approaches, methods, strategies, and techniques may be used at any level, the materials have been selected for use by students in grades five through nine and are so noted in interest and reading levels. The titles may, in fact, be appropriate for older readers as well. Grades five through nine represent a period of development during which many students become lost and begin to lose faith in reading as a way of finding answers and gaining satisfaction.

Each book in the series is meant to provide one method in beginning an exploration with students. One would not expect every approach to work with every individual. Nor would one expect every teacher and library media specialist to enjoy or feel comfortable with every approach. Each approach is an option.

Finally, the sources and materials suggested in the series were selected given a number of criteria:

- General literary quality and accuracy;
- Availability;
- Readability and interest levels;
- Ethnic, racial, and sex-role representation;
- Availability of media support materials; and
- Recommendations in selected journals and guides.

It is the hope of the author that the suggested books and materials will serve as stimuli for grouping literature in attractive packages. Perhaps each package will tempt some reader to open the book and turn the page.

Paula Kay Montgomery

Preface

In *Exploring New Methods for Collecting Students' School-Based Writing: NAEP's 1990 Portfolio Study,* Claudia A. Gentile reports on the types of writing students must do—stories, reports, essays, and persuasive pieces. All of these forms (i.e., narrative, expository, persuasive, procedural, and descriptive writing) are among the types of literary forms discussed in *Approaches to Literature through Literary Forms.* The emphasis on students' ability to communicate effectively relates back to the ability to read and understand these forms. Student motivation to read and use all of these literary forms is the focus of this book.

There are many reasons for reading, and readers have come to expect certain literary forms to meet a given need. By attending to and recognizing the structure and purpose of literature, teachers and library media specialists can introduce students to the many types of literature from which they have to choose.

The advantage of the literary forms approach is that it emphasizes structure, which can be matched to students' reasons for reading. It would be a mistake, however, for classroom teachers or library media specialists to try only this approach with students. In a well-rounded reading program, a literary forms approach should be used in conjunction with others, such as thematic, genre, author, chronological, subject, or skills approaches. Parents and other reading volunteers might be called upon to help in this endeavor.

A literary forms approach reflects the hope that an emphasis on structure will bring the comfort and familiarity many students need to "click" with a particular topic. Therefore, the lists of resources in the chapters often will contain television programs, films, and videotapes in addition to books and articles. Some of these resources may be considered outside the realm of educational materials, but the materials were suggested because, in fact, students are learning outside the "educational setting." Movies and television are at least as powerful motivators as what students see and hear in classrooms. Many films and television programs form the basis of conversations among students. Selections are aimed at the middle school group of readers, grades five through eight, and the adults who work with them.

After the overview in chapter one, the book is organized by the literary forms themselves. Each chapter defines a form and provides subforms. Activities are suggested for each subform. Please note that some suggestions challenge readers to take risks. For example, the activity on mythology does not use the safer "Greek gods," but instead has been developed around myths still shared in Indonesian cultures. Such activities encourage teachers and library media specialists to think about the literary form itself and allow students to read widely within the form. Bibliographic materials are also suggested for further reading.

Before inviting readers to browse these chapters, a special thanks is in order. First, "thanks" goes to the professionals in libraries and library media centers in Maryland. Under the leadership of Maurice Travillian, assistant state superintendent for library development and services, the libraries have amassed accessible holdings connected through the Maryland Interlibrary Loan Agency. Titles and materials included here were located using the Maryland Internet gopher, Sailor. Also a special "thank you" is offered to H. Thomas Walker in Howard County Public Schools for his help in obtaining professional resources and hints about other resources.

APPROACHES TO LITERATURE THROUGH LITERARY FORM

Literary Forms

"Communication may be made in broken words, the business of life be carried on with substantives alone; but that is not what we call literature; and the true business of the literary artist is to plait or weave his meaning, involving it around itself; so that each sentence, by successive phrases, shall first come into a kind of a knot, and then, after a moment of suspended meaning, solve and clear itself." These were the thoughts of Robert Louis Stevenson as he discussed the patterns of writers in "On Some Technical Elements of Style," *The Art of Writing*. The analogy of authors as weavers conjures up the patterns authors create, the woven knots that can ensnare the adolescent reader. Just as weavers have developed their own conventions and patterns, writers have developed structural conventions, sets of ritualized written devices that allow the communicator to send messages in forms to which the listener has become accustomed.

Although people are often unaware of the process, their ability to recognize literary forms makes communication easier. Familiarity with these structures allows the audience to pay more attention to the content of the message. Form provides a cultural and literary schema for signaling the purpose of communication. When the communicator says, "Once upon a time," the phrase signals a story, a narrative. The listener knows that a message with a beginning, a middle, and an end is about to be begin. If the listener has experienced many pleasurable moments with this type of message, he or she is likely to listen with anticipation. Many other frameworks of written language have developed over time. These frameworks, structures, or literary forms are clearly present in the writing that students will encounter. As such, they may also become organizers for presenting reading experiences to students. Literary forms become another method for grouping literature into meaningful units of study.

With a literary forms approach, structure is used to define the reading experience for students. Literary forms are the structures that have come to be associated with certain communication purposes. They begin with the basic phonemes and proceed to words, sentences, paragraphs, and groups of paragraphs. One example of a literary form is the diary, a written device for recording personal thoughts. Diaries are usually recognizable because they are in chronological order, written in first person, and include sentence fragments. In many cases, diaries include descriptions of events as well as musings on their meanings. Any younger brother or sister who has tried to sneak a peek at a sibling's diary understands and recognizes the purpose of the form, usually to the great annoyance of the diarist. Literary form relies heavily on purpose and language structure. An instructional unit that uses a literary form for grouping students' reading comprehension experiences would naturally address the purpose of written language.

A literary forms approach to literature differs from thematic, subject, author, skills, chronological, and genre approaches. An approach based on literary forms does not necessarily include books and materials that share a common theme, as in the thematic approach, or deal with the same subject, as in the subject approach to literature. And the first priority of the literary forms approach is not the comparison of works of one author or several authors, as in an author approach. In the literary forms approach, the readers' skills that are emphasized are those related to understanding how the form provides clues to meaning. In a skills approach, however, one might find several types of literary forms, such as exposition, description, and narrative grouped together to teach students about the concepts of main idea and supporting idea. The literary forms approach does not address the order or development of the work of an author or groups of authors, as in the chronological approach. Finally, a genre approach includes a partial emphasis on form, but it differs from a pure literary forms approach because genre focuses on subject as well as form. Historical fiction novels illustrate the difference. Novels are literary forms, but there are many variations of the novel. Historical fiction novels are a genre because they share a common subject. Novels appear in other genres such as fantasy, mystery, westerns, or science fiction. The literary forms approach, on the other hand, encompasses all subjects because the emphasis is on structure alone. Such an approach allows the teacher to include many themes, subjects, or authors to appeal to the many interests of the students.

THE ELEMENTS OF DISCOURSE

The literary forms approach relies on the discourse itself. Discourse is connected speech, without regard to length, that sends a coherent message unified in meaning. Discourse includes semantics, syntax, coherence, and organization and structure.

Semantics, or word meanings, become important in conveying the message within each form. They are the blocks with which a literary forms approach is built. Words change meanings and nuance with the form. Word meanings convey temporal and spatial relationships and can be modified, expanded, or contracted. Alliteration, attribute, colloquialism, contract, dialect, dialectical expression, expand, figurative language, hyperbole, idiom, irony, metaphor, onomatopoeia, paradox, personification, and simile are part of the way in which we describe word meanings. If a literary forms approach were concentrating on plays, we might expect to pay attention to the semantics that provide meaning. Dialogue might be an area of concentration in a unit of study.

Syntax is also important in a literary forms approach. Syntax is the arrangement of words in phrases, clauses, and sentences, or sentence structure. In the English language, sentences consist of linear sequences of words, one following the other in space and time. Word order shows relationships among words. Made up of morphemes (the smallest identifiable units with constant meaning or grammatical function), words become part of phrases (words centered on a core element called the head that is grammatically coherent). Clauses are larger units, consisting of phrases, that specify relationships among various participants, each identified by a noun phrase and playing a certain role in the clause. A sentence with one clause is simple; a sentence with more than one clause is complex. Sentence structure provides meaning or shows relationships between actors and action. The skill with which authors arrange and combine clauses, produce sentences, and organize sentences into a coherent work determines the success of the communication.

An added dimension for the study of literary form is coherence, or the sense that words make within the language's syntactic rules. Rules allow for an infinite number of combinations. How has the author strung words together within the context of these rules to communicate an idea? Are the sentences simple or complex? Does this organization fit the purpose of the message to be conveyed? Why is one author more successful in a given form than another? The syntactic variations in each literary form are often apparent in the relationships between sentences and series of sentences, which is known as coherence. Such relationships may be temporal, locative, comparative, causal, conditional, or logical. Terms such as *locative* and *temporal* help describe coherence. Each literary form varies in coherence. Some forms, such as exposition, rely on more obvious relationships between sentences, whereas others, such as description, rely on more subtle ones. The purpose of the form is seen in syntax, action, actor, ellipsis, goal, intonation, juncture, noun phrase, pitch, pronominal referent, reiteration, root sentence, stress, or verb phrase.

Finally, organization and structure describe the relationships between groups of sentences. Different types of discourse have unique structural elements that affect meaning. For example, sentences are organized differently for relating procedures or directions than they are for telling a story, although both discourses may be sequential. Organization and structure show the relationships between content, form or medium, message and speaker's intent, physical and social context, and audience's purposes.

TYPES OF LITERARY FORMS

Literary forms may best be defined in terms of the purpose of the speaker's or author's communication and the likely content of the communication. Five types of discourse or categories of literary forms have evolved over thousands of years. These are narration and drama, exposition, persuasion or argumentation, procedure, and description. (Some consider drama as a sixth discreet form.) Each of these forms includes a number of subordinate forms.

Narrative Writing

Literary forms may best be defined in terms of the purpose of the speaker's or author's communication and the likely content of the communication. Generally, narration is considered to be a telling, retelling, or an account of an event or series of events that occur in a given setting over a period of time. In other words, a narrative is a story that has a sequence of events leading to some kind of ending. Narration reflects a certain point of view, such as first person or third person omniscient or specific. Usually characters motivate the reader, who becomes involved in their actions. Most often, a narrative is meant to entertain, although it can instruct and inform through example. There are many examples of narration, including autobiographies, ballads, biographies, diaries and journals, fables, folktales, legends, myths, nonsense verse and rhymes, novels, short narratives as found in certain picture books and I-Can-Read stories, short stories, and story poems or epics.

Drama may be considered narrative, although it is often considered separately because action and events are re-created by actors playing roles. Again, the purpose is most often entertainment, but examples may inform or instruct. Drama includes skits and plays, dramatic readings, monologues, dialogues, operas and musicals, and even mime.

Expository Writing

Exposition presents information or ideas for a reader's consideration. It may explain, state cause and effect, compare and contrast, define, chronicle, generalize, or summarize. The reader encounters main ideas supported by details. Often these main ideas are written as topic sentences found at the beginning, middle, or end of paragraphs, but just as often, the main idea must be inferred from the details. Expository writing appeals to the reader's sense of logic and satisfies curiosity. The ubiquitous expository form is found in articles, reports, text in instructional materials, essays, letters, and factual books often categorized as nonfiction. Although much exposition has had a "bad rap," it is in fact a very satisfying form for young people. Intended to impart information quickly, exposition helps fill in gaps in knowledge about the "real world." Depending on the subject of the expository passage, students can become involved in knowing more about their environment.

Persuasive Writing

Persuasion or argumentation presents two or more different views about an idea or issue. In persuasive writing, the author introduces a view, supports the view, and draws a conclusion. The purpose of persuasive writing is to convince the reader about the position that has been taken. The author uses language that will capture the audience's opinions, values, and beliefs. Persuasive writing is often combined with other forms but may be found on its own in political speeches, sermons, advertisements, debates, editorials, and informal arguments.

Procedural Writing

Through logically sequenced directions, procedural writing tells the reader how to do something. Procedures are intended to meet the reader's need to complete a particular task. In procedural writing, the author often addresses the reader in second person or with commands. The use of second person and sequencing can make such writing deceptively simple, but incredibly difficult to comprehend. Procedures are found as recipes, directions or instructions in manuals and forms, and experiments.

Descriptive Writing

Description is another literary form usually found combined with other types of writing. The purpose of descriptive writing is to convey sensory details and to elicit a response to those details from the reader. The author relies on the reader's past experiences. When found on its own, description is usually in the form of descriptive poetry, catalog descriptions, or travelogues.

ORIGINS AND MOTIVATIONAL INFLUENCES

The origins of these literary forms are difficult to determine. Most forms, especially the narrative, predate written language. Who knows when the first story was told? When did the first individual try to explain how to make an object like a stone arrow or weapon? Who was the first person to share observations about the environment? The study of communication, language, and writing gives clues to origins. Clay tables, writings on stone, and fragile scrolls include evidence of narration in the form of stories; exposition in the form of inventories; and description in the form of poetry, procedures for collecting taxes, and even opinions of rulers.

For students, what becomes important in a study of literary forms is the author's purpose. The words, sentences, and paragraphs in each literary form vary based on the author's intent. Structure, because it has evolved to support purpose, becomes a clue as to what to expect from a piece of writing. The reader senses the author's purpose in the written clues and becomes motivated if that purpose strikes a chord. For example, if students enjoy finding out how other individuals have dealt with life, they may find biographies extremely satisfying, especially if they discover that they have something in common with the subject of the biography.

Although literary forms are often not motivators by themselves, they can help structure an approach to literature that provides comfort to adolescents who are reading for a specific reason. Adolescents vary in their abilities as readers or nonreaders. For example, students may go through periods in which the rhyme or riddle is of great appeal. If a reader finds satisfaction in that particular purpose, the form will be motivating. The teacher or library media specialist who deliberately considers the purpose of writing and collects and groups materials according to that purpose will find a wider knowledge and consideration of literary forms to be an asset. It is as natural for students to want to read and use "how-to" books as it is for them to read articles on nature. There is comfort in understanding that you can complete a task or find out how to do something if you follow a set of instructions.

Helping students become familiar with the different types of literary forms is a gift. The different literary forms give readers options for fitting purposes to their reading efforts. Teachers or library media specialists can serve their clientele well if they introduce and promote reading of all forms.

Professional Sources

The in-depth study of language, syntax, and linguistics is beyond the scope of this book. However, there are many sources for background information and further research into discourse analysis and structure. Search library catalogs and databases under a diverse set of terms such as *literary form, literary genre, literary devices, structural analysis, syntax, text analysis, discourse analysis,* and *language patterns.* As literary forms of interest are identified, the terms for specific forms, such as *expository writing* or *biography,* will also yield information. The following materials may be useful in beginning such a study.

Ajay, Helen. *Literary Genres and Style.* Los Alamitos, CA: Southwest Regional Laboratory for Educational Research and Development, 1974. ED 216377.

Babcock, Robert Witbeck, Robert Dewey Horn, and Thomas Hopkins English. *Creative Writing for College Students: A Summary of the Theory of Exposition, Argument, Narrative, and Description.* New York: American Book Company, 1938.

Bach, Emmon. *Syntactic Theory*. Washington, DC: University Press of America, 1982.

Baker, C. L. *English Syntax*. Cambridge, MA: M.I.T. Press, 1989.

Beetz, Kirk H., and Suzanne Niemeyer. *Guide to Literature and Biography for Young Adults*. Washington, DC: Beacham Publishing, 1989.

Birch, David. *Language, Literature and Critical Practice: Ways of Analysing Text*. New York: Routledge, 1989.

Borsley, Robert D. *Syntactic Theory: A Unified Approach*. New York: Edward Arnold, 1991.

Brown, Gillian, and George Yule. *Discourse Analysis*. London: Cambridge University Press, 1983.

Burke, Kenneth. *The Philosophy of Literary Form: Studies in Symbolic Action*. Baton Rouge, LA: Louisiana State University Press, 1967.

Campbell, Karlyn Kohrs, and Kathleen Hall Jamieson, eds. *Form and Genre: Shaping Rhetorical Action*. 1978. ED 151893.

Canary, Robert H., and Henry Kozicki. *The Writing of History: Literary Form and Historical Understanding*. Madison, WI: University of Wisconsin Press, 1978.

Carter, Ronald, and Deirdre Burton, eds. *Literary Text and Language Study*. London: Edward Arnold, 1982.

Chomsky, Noam. *Aspects of the Theory of Syntax, and Knowledge of Language*. Cambridge, MA: M.I.T. Press, 1986.

———. *Language and Mind*. New York: Harcourt Brace Jovanovich, 1972.

———. *The Logical Structure of Linguistic Theory*. Chicago: University of Chicago Press, 1985.

———. *Syntactic Structures*. The Hague: Mouton, 1957.

Coulthard, Malcolm. *An Introduction to Discourse Analysis*. London: Longman, 1977.

Culicover, Peter. *Syntax*. New York: Academic Press, 1976.

Cummings, Melodie. *Literature Line-Up: A Study of Different Forms of Literature for Intermediate Grade Children*. Cedar Falls, IA: Area Education Agency 7, 1980. ED 239205.

Davies, Andrew. "Write On (Teaching Students to Write in a Variety of Genres)." *Times Educational Supplement* 3820 (September 15, 1989), pp. 30.

Dillon, George L. *Constructing Texts: Elements of a Theory of Composition and Style*. Bloomington, IN: Indiana University Press, 1981.

———. *Language Processing and the Reading of Literature: Toward a Model of Comprehension*. Bloomington, IN: Indiana University Press, 1978.

Dyson, A. E. *Between Two Worlds: Aspects of Literary Form*. New York: St. Martin's Press, 1972.

Foley, William A., and Robert Van Valin. *Functional Syntax and Universal Grammar*. New York: Cambridge University Press, 1984.

Form, Genre. Northbrook, IL: Anthony Roland Collection of Films on Art, 1989. 1 videocassette. 25 min.

Fowler, Alastair. *Kinds of Literature: An Introduction to the Theory of Genres and Modes.* Cambridge, MA: Harvard University Press, 1982.

Giordano, Gerard. "Using Language Structure to Teach Adolescents and Adults to Read." *Reading Improvement* 15, no. 1 (Spring 1978), pp. 13–19.

Hernadi, Paul. "The Aims of Discourse Revisited: Reading and Writing beyond Genre." *ADE Bulletin* 88 (Winter 1988), pp. 27–29.

———. *Beyond Genre: New Directions in Literary Classification.* Ithaca, NY: Cornell University Press, 1972.

Horowitz, Rosalind, and S. Jay Samuels. *Comprehending Oral and Written Language.* San Diego, CA: Academic Press, 1987.

Kinneavy, James L., John Q. Cope, and J. W. Campbell. *Aims and Audiences in Writing.* Dubuque, IA: Kendall/Hunt Publishing Co., 1976.

Literature: Internal Forms. Atlanta, GA: Regional Curriculum Project, 1986. ED 042744.

Literature: Internal Forms. Atlanta, GA: Regional Curriculum Project, 1968. ED 042744

Littlefair, Alison B. "Register Awareness: An Important Factor in Children's Continuing Reading Development." *Reading* 23, no. 2 (July 1989), pp. 56–61.

McCarthy, Michael. *Discourse Analysis for Language Teachers.* New York: Cambridge University Press, 1991.

Martin, J. R. *English Text: System and Structure.* Philadelphia: John Benjamins Publishing Co., 1992.

Moffett, James. *A Student-Centered Language Arts Curriculum, Grades K–13: A Handbook for Teachers.* Boston: Houghton Mifflin, 1973.

———. *Teaching the Universe of Discourse.* Boston: Houghton Mifflin, 1983.

Moffett, James, and Betty Jane Wagner. *Student-Centered Language Arts, K–12.* Portsmouth, NH: Boynton/Cook Publishers, 1992.

Prince, Michael B. "Literacy and Genre: Towards a Pedagogy of Mediation." *College English* 51, no. 7 (November 1989), pp. 730–50.

Quellmalz, Edys, and Frank Capell. *Defining Writing Domains: Effects of Discourse and Response Mode.* Los Angeles, CA: Center for the Study of Evaluation, 1979. ED 212661.

Radford, Andrew. *Syntactic Theory and the Acquisition of English Syntax: The Nature of Early Child Grammars of English.* Cambridge, MA: Blackwell, 1990.

———. *Transformational Grammar: A First Course.* New York: Cambridge University Press, 1985.

———. *Transformational Syntax.* New York: Cambridge University Press, 1981.

Reavley, Kate. *Connecting Two Aims of Discourse: The Literary and the Expressive.* Paper presented at the annual meeting of the Conference on College Composition and Communication, Detroit, MI, March 17–19, 1983. ED 230958.

Rietz, Sandra A. *A Comparison of Certain Structural Characteristics of Language Selections Representing Both Oral and Written Thought and Purpose.* Doctoral dissertation, University of Colorado at Boulder, 1976. ED 140301.

Roberts, Paul. *Patterns of English.* New York: Harcourt Brace, 1956.

Rochemont, Michael S. *A Theory of Stylistic Rules in English.* New York: Garland Publishing, 1985.

Sherrard, Carol. "Developing Discourse Analysis." *Journal of General Psychology* 118, no. 2 (April 1991), pp. 171–79.

Shuman, Amy. *Storytelling Rights: The Uses of Oral and Written Texts by Urban Adolescents.* New York: Cambridge University Press, 1986.

Singer, Murray. "Global Inferences of Text Situations." *Discourse Processes* 16, nos. 1–2 (January-June 1993), pp. 161–68.

Stockwell, Robert P. *Foundations of Syntactic Theory.* Englewood Cliffs, NJ: Prentice-Hall, 1977.

Strelka, Joseph P. *Theories of Literary Genre.* University Park, PA: Pennsylvania State University Press, 1978.

Stubbs, Michael. *Discourse Analysis: The Sociolinguistic Analysis of Natural Language.* Chicago: University of Chicago Press, 1983.

Toolan, Michael. *Language, Text and Context: Essays in Stylistics.* New York: Routledge, 1992.

Traugott, Elizabeth Closs. *A History of English Syntax: A Transformational Approach to the History of English Sentence Structure.* New York: Holt, Rinehart and Winston, 1972.

Ventola, Eija, ed. *Approaches to the Analysis of Literary Discourse.* Pargas, Finland: Abo Academy Press, 1991. ED 358687.

Wallace-Crabbe, Chris. *Falling into Language.* New York: Oxford University Press, 1990.

Wason-Ellam, Linda. "Using Literary Patterns: Who's in Control of the Authorship?" *Language Arts* 65, no. 3 (March 1988), pp. 291–303.

Widdowson, H. G. *Teaching Language as Communication.* Oxford: Oxford University Press, 1983.

DEVELOPMENT OF A LITERARY FORMS APPROACH

There are many ways to introduce students to books and materials by literary form besides simply collecting materials in a particular form. A logical beginning would be consideration of the options open in order to select logical matches that relate to or follow the selected form. What are methods, strategies, and techniques and how can matches be made?

The term *method* defines how the teacher or library media specialist concentrates on the behavior of the individual using the literature. The leader uses methods or engages in generalized behavior patterns to introduce information or structure learning. The term *method* refers to the application of principles, practices, and procedures that can be transferred often to more than one area of interest or study.

Techniques are more specific ways of presenting instructional material or conducting instructional activities. For example, a method of instruction is the discussion, but there are more detailed techniques for setting up and developing a panel discussion, and there are different kinds of discussions. Techniques refer to the specific skills embedded within the method, such as how to pace the discussion with open-ended or probing questions.

A *strategy* is the plan or the means by which the method might be used. The strategy includes the many other considerations necessary for successfully using a method. For example, how students might be grouped, the arrangement of the learning area for using the method, or the use of specific behaviors to elicit response might be included in the strategy for using a method to motivate reading. A discussion technique might be used with a plan to provide plenty of "wait time" during certain types of open-ended questions when a question is asked. This might be part of the strategy to enable students to think about the material they read.

Many of the methods, techniques, and strategies are actually related to literary forms. For example, demonstration is a common method for teaching. The nature of the method is aligned to the learning of sequential tasks. Demonstrations could easily be combined with procedural reading and writing activities. Audiovisual materials appeal to the senses, especially sight and sound. Descriptive writing would therefore be a good supplement to these resources. Lyrical poetry could be related to song and dance. Journal writing, which has become a popular way to teach and reinforce students' reading and writing skills, might be combined with the reading of autobiographies, diaries, and journals.

Review the following list of methods, strategies, and techniques and consider which might be used with certain literary forms, although not necessarily limited to them.

Methods, Strategies, and Techniques

Art Methods
Illustration
  (various media formats)
Model Making
  Models
  Dioramas
  Mock-Ups
Sculpture
  Clay
  Stone
  Papier Mâché
Textiles
  Fabrics
  Tapestries
Bulletin Boards/Displays
Crafts

Audiovisual Methods (Production and Use)
Sound
  Listening Activities
  Taped Radio Programs
Visual
  Charts
  Graphics
  Flannel Board
  Microfilm
  Visual Activities
  Posters
  Animation
Sound Visual
  Film
  Sound Filmstrip
  Videotape
  Slide/Tape
Interactive
  Computer Drills
  Simulations and Games
  Databases (CD-ROM and
    Laser Disc)
Sound Visual Interactive
Tactile
  Manipulative
Sound Visual Interactive
Tactile

Brainstorming

Conversation

Dance
Dance Forms (i.e., modern,
  ballet, folk dancing, etc.)

Debate

Demonstration

Directed Learning
Learning Activity Package
Directed Reading Activity
Concept Guides
Structured Overviews
Guided Reading
Paired Reading/Learning
Contracts
Learning Centers
Language Experience
  Approach
Behavior Modification
Programmed Learning
Graphic Organizers

Discussion
Guided Discussion
Exploratory Discussion
Panel Discussion
General Discussion

Drama
Sociodrama
Role Play
Play
Costuming
Creative Dramatics

Methods, Strategies, and Techniques-cont'd.

Drama—Cont'd.
   Puppetry (marionettes, hand
      puppets, shadow puppets,
      etc.)
   Mime
   Storytelling
   Reading Aloud
   Choral Reading
   Reenactment
   Readers Theater
   Story Theater

Field Trip

Game
   Gaming
   Simulations

Inquiry Method (Discovery)
   Scientific Method (Investiga-
      tion)
   Puzzles
   Research Methods/Strategies
   Simulation
   Individual Study
   Laboratory Experiment
   Do-Look-and-Learn
   Problem Solving

Lecture
   Speech Making
   Book Talk
   Book Report

Music
   Song Writing
   Listening to Music
   Musical Drama

Questioning
   Question/Discussion/Evalua-
      tion
   Interview
   Oral History
   Author
   Survey

Reading
   Sustained Silent Reading
   Free Reading
   Browsing
   Cooperative Reading

Writing Methods
   Diary/Journal Writing
   Writing in Literary Forms
   Word Processing

LOCATION AND SELECTION OF STUDENT MATERIALS

Published bibliographies do not usually group books and reading materials by literary form, and those that do are often uneven in their representation. Some types of literary forms, such as myths or legends, are listed in guides, but procedural materials or persuasive writings are more difficult to find. Sometimes bibliographies group materials under such categories as folktales. Myths, legends, folktales, and even epic poetry and story poems might be found under such a heading.

   The following general list of selection tools includes bibliographies of recommended books that appeal to grades five through eight. Astute teachers or library media specialists will understand the nature of the literary form and will find these titles useful in locating types of materials.

These selection sources or annotated bibliographies are arranged alphabetically by author. An effort was made to limit this list to those sources published after 1984 unless the title included examples of forms that might be useful. Sources that may yield specific forms are noted. This list is not meant to be comprehensive. Instead, bibliographies and selection sources that approach collection development from different angles (including age, race, gender, and media format) are included.

AAAS Science Book List, 1978–1985. Washington, DC: American Association for the Advancement of Science, 1986.
Includes expository and procedural forms primarily.

American Reference Books Annual. Littleton, CO: Libraries Unlimited, 1970-present. Annual.
Includes exposition primarily.

Anatomy of Wonder: A Critical Guide to Science Fiction. New York: R. R. Bowker, 1987.
Includes narration with emphasis on the novel.

Audiocassette Finder: A Subject Guide to Educational and Literary Materials on Audiocassettes. Medford, NJ: Plexus Publishers, 1989.
Includes all forms.

AudioVideo Review Digest. Detroit: Gale Research, 1989-present. Quarterly.
Includes all forms.

AV Market Place. New York: R. R. Bowker, 1984-present. Annual.
Includes all forms.

Barron, Neil, Wayne Barton, Kristin Ramsdell, and Steven A. Stilwell. *What Do I Read Next?* Detroit: Gale Research, 1993.
Includes narration primarily.

Bauer, Caroline Feller. *Read for the Fun of It.* New York: H. W. Wilson, 1991.
Includes all forms.

Best Books for Children: Preschool through Middle Grades. New York: R. R. Bowker, 1985.
Includes all forms with emphasis on narration.

Best Books for Junior High Readers. New York: R. R. Bowker, 1991.
Includes narration primarily.

Best Books for Senior High Readers. New York: R. R. Bowker, 1991.
Includes narration primarily.

Best Books for Young Adults. Chicago: American Library Association. Annual.
Includes all forms.

Biagini, Mary K. *A Handbook of Contemporary Fiction for Public Libraries and School Libraries.* Metuchen, NJ: Scarecrow Press, 1989.
Includes narration primarily.

The Black Experience in Children's Books. New York: New York Public Library, 1989.
Includes narration primarily.

Blackburn, G. Meredith, III. *Index to Poetry for Children and Young People, 1982–1987*. New York: H. W. Wilson, 1989.
See earlier editions also. Includes narration and description.

Bodart, Joni Richards. *Booktalk! 2: Booktalking for All Ages and Audiences*. New York: H. W. Wilson, 1985.
Includes narration primarily.

————. *Booktalk! 4: Selections from the Booktalker for All Ages and Audiences*. New York: H. W. Wilson, 1992.
Includes narration primarily.

————. *Booktalk! 5*. New York: H. W. Wilson, 1993.
Includes narration primarily.

Bodart-Talbot, Joni. *Booktalk! 3: More Booktalks for All Ages*. New York: H. W. Wilson, 1988.
Includes primarily narration.

Book Links: Connecting Books, Libraries and Classrooms. Chicago: American Library Association, 1991-present. Bimonthly.
Includes all forms.

The Book Report. Worthington, OH: Linworth Publishing, 1982-present. Bimonthly.
Includes all forms.

The Book Review Digest. New York: H. W. Wilson, 1905-present. Quarterly.
Includes all forms.

BookBrain, Grades 4–6. Phoenix, AZ: Oryx Press, 1993. Apple or IBM computer program.
Includes narration primarily.

BookBrain, Grades 7–9. Phoenix, AZ: Oryx Press, 1990. Apple or IBM computer program.
Includes narration primarily.

The Bookfinder: A Guide to Children's Literature about the Needs and Problems of Youth, Vol. 1. Circle Pines, MN: American Guidance Service, 1977.
Includes narration primarily.

The Bookfinder, Vol. 2: A Guide to Children's Literature about the Needs and Problems of Youth Aged 2–15: Annotations of Books Published 1975–1978. Circle Pines, MN: American Guidance Service, 1981.
Includes narration primarily.

The Bookfinder, Vol. 4. Circle Pines, MN: American Guidance Service, 1989.
Includes narration primarily.

The Bookfinder: When Kids Need Books: Annotations of Books Published 1979 through 1982. Circle Pines, MN: American Guidance Service, 1982.
Includes narration primarily.

Booklist. Chicago: American Library Association. 22 issues per year.
Includes all forms.

Books for the Teen Age. New York: New York Public Library, 1929-present. Annual.
Includes narration primarily.

Brady, William O. *Guide to Popular U.S. Government Publications.* Littleton, CO: Libraries Unlimited, 1990.
Includes exposition primarily.

Carruth, Gordon. *The Young Reader's Companion.* New York: R. R. Bowker, 1993.
Includes all forms.

Carter, Betty, and Richard F. Abrahamson. *Nonfiction for Young Adults: From Delight to Wisdom.* Phoenix, AZ: Oryx Press, 1990.
Includes all forms.

Children's Fiction, 1876–1984. New York: R. R. Bowker, 1986.
Includes narration primarily.

Choice. Chicago: Association of College and Research Libraries/American Library Association, 1964-present. 11 issues per year.
Includes all forms.

Cordier, Mary Hurlburt, and Maria A. Perez-Stable. *Peoples of the American West: Historical Perspectives through Children's Literature.* Metuchen, NJ: Scarecrow Press, 1989.
Includes narration and exposition primarily.

Criscoe, Betty, and Philip J. Lanasa III. *Award-Winning Books for Children and Young Adults: An Annual Guide, 1989.* Metuchen, NJ: Scarecrow Press, 1990.
Includes all forms with emphasis on narration.

Criscoe, Betty, and Philip J. Lanasa III. *Award-Winning Books for Children and Young Adults, 1990–1991.* Metuchen, NJ: Scarecrow Press, 1993.
Includes all forms.

Dame, Melvina Azar. *Serving Linguistically and Culturally Diverse Students: Strategies for the School Library Media Specialist.* New York: Neal-Schuman, 1993.
Includes all forms.

Easy Reading: Book Series and Periodicals for Less Able Readers. Newark, DE: International Reading Association, 1989.
Includes narration and exposition.

Educational Film and Video Locator. New York: R. R. Bowker, 1992.
Includes all forms.

Egoff, Sheila A. *Worlds Within: Children's Fantasy from the Middle Ages to Today.* Chicago: American Library Association, 1988.
Includes all forms.

Ekhaml, Letitia T., and Lice J. Wittig. *U. S. Government Publications for the School Library Media Center.* Littleton, CO: Libraries Unlimited, 1991.
Includes exposition and procedural forms primarily.

The Elementary School Library Collection: A Guide to Books and Other Media, Phases 1-2-3. Williamsport, PA: Brodart, 1994. Print or CD-ROM versions available.
Includes all forms.

The Emergency Librarian. Seattle, WA: Dyad Services, 1973-present. 5 issues per year.
  Includes all forms.
The English Journal. Urbana, IL: National Council for Teachers of English. 8 issues per year.
  Includes all forms.
Estes, Sally. *Genre Favorites for Young Adults.* Chicago: American Library Association, 1993.
  Includes narration with emphasis on the novel.
————. *Popular Reading for Children III: A Collection of Booklist Columns.* Chicago: American Library Association, 1992.
  Includes narration primarily.
Ettlinger, John R. T., and Diana L. Spirt. *Choosing Books for Young People: A Guide to Criticism and Bibliography, 1976–1984.* Vols. 1 and 2. Chicago: American Library Association, 1982; Phoenix, AZ: Oryx Press, 1987.
  Includes all forms.
Exploring the Great Lakes States through Literature. Phoenix, AZ: Oryx Press, 1994.
  Includes all forms.
Exploring the Mountain States through Literature. Phoenix, AZ: Oryx Press, 1994.
  Includes all forms.
Exploring the Northeast States through Literature. Phoenix, AZ: Oryx Press, 1994.
  Includes all forms.
Exploring the Pacific States through Literature. Phoenix, AZ: Oryx Press, 1994.
  Includes all forms.
Exploring the Plains States through Literature. Phoenix, AZ: Oryx Press, 1994.
  Includes all forms.
Exploring the Southeast States through Literature. Phoenix, AZ: Oryx Press, 1994.
  Includes all forms.
Exploring the Southwest States through Literature. Phoenix, AZ: Oryx Press, 1994.
  Includes all forms.
Fantasy Literature for Children and Young Adults: An Annotated Bibliography. New York: R. R. Bowker, 1988.
  Includes narration primarily, with emphasis on the fantasy novel.
Feminist Resources for Schools and Colleges: A Guide to Curricular Materials. New York: The Feminist Press, 1986.
  Includes all forms.
Fiction Catalog. New York: H. W. Wilson, 1991. 1 hardbound volume with 4 annual supplements.
  Includes narration primarily.
Film and Video Finder. Medford, NJ: Plexus Publishing, 1989.
  Includes all forms.
Free Resource Builder for Librarians and Teachers. Jefferson, NC: McFarland, 1986.
  Includes all forms.

Friedberg, Joan Brest, June B. Mullins, and Adleaide Weir Sukiennik. *Portraying Persons with Disabilities: An Annotated Bibliography of Nonfiction for Children and Teenagers.* New York: R. R. Bowker, 1992.
Includes exposition, persuasion, and procedural forms.

Gerhardstein, Virginia Brokaw. *Dickinson's American Historical Fiction.* Metuchen, NJ: Scarecrow Press, 1986.
Includes narration with emphasis on the historical novel.

Gillespie, John T. *The Junior High School Paperback Collection.* Chicago: American Library Association, 1985.
Includes narration primarily.

Gillespie, John T., and Corinne J. Naden. *Seniorplots: A Book Talk Guide for Use with Readers Ages 15–18.* By John T. Gillespie and Corinne J. Naden. New York: R. R. Bowker, 1989.
Includes narration primarily.

Growing Up Is Hard to Do. Chicago: American Library Association, 1994.
Includes all forms.

Hauser, Paula, and Gail A. Nelson. *Books for the Gifted Child, Volume 2.* New York: R. R. Bowker, 1988.
Includes all forms.

Health Education. Reston, VA: American Alliance for Health, Physical Education, and Recreation, 1975-present. Bimonthly.
Includes all forms.

Her Way: A Guide to Biographies of Women for Young People. Chicago: American Library Association, 1984.
Includes narration with emphasis on biography.

Hi/Lo Handbook: Books, Materials and Services for the Problem Reader. New York: R. R. Bowker, 1985.
Includes all forms.

Hit List: Frequently Challenged Young Adult Titles. Chicago: Young Adult Library Services Association/American Library Association, 1989.
Includes all forms.

Horn Book Guide. Boston: The Horn Book, Inc., 1989-present. Semiannual.
Includes all forms.

Horn Book Magazine. Boston: The Horn Book, Inc. 6 issues yearly.
Includes all forms.

Howard, Elizabeth F. *America as Story: Historical Fiction for Secondary Schools.* Chicago: American Library Association, 1988.
Includes narration with emphasis on the novel.

How-To: 1400 Best Books on Doing Almost Anything. New York: R. R. Bowker, 1984.
Includes procedural forms.

Index to Collective Biographies for Young Readers. New York: R. R. Bowker, 1988.
Includes narration with emphasis on biography.

Index to Fairy Tales, 1978–1986, Including Folklore, Legends, and Myths in Collections. Metuchen, NJ: Scarecrow Press, 1989. Earlier editions available.
Includes narration with emphasis on myth, folktale, legend, and fable.

Introducing Bookplots 3: A Book Talk Guide for Use with Readers Ages 8–12. New York: R. R. Bowker, 1988.
Includes narration primarily.

Introducing Books: A Guide for the Middle Grades. New York: R. R. Bowker, 1970.
Includes narration primarily.

Jacob, Merle, and Hope Apple. *To Be Continued: An Annotated Guide to Sequels.* Phoenix, AZ: Oryx Press, 1995.
Includes narration.

Jensen, Julie M., and Nancy L. Roser. *Adventuring with Books: A Booklist for Pre-K–Grade 6.* Urbana, IL: National Council of Teachers of English, 1993.
Includes narration primarily.

Jim Kobak's Kirkus Reviews. New York: Kirkus Service, 1985-present. Semiannual.
Includes all forms.

Journal of Reading. Newark, DE: International Reading Association, 1956-present. Monthly.
Includes all forms.

Journal of Youth Services in Libraries. Chicago: Association for Library Service to Children and Young Adult Services, Division of the American Library Association, 1987-present. Quarterly. Includes all forms.

Junior High School Catalog. New York: H. W. Wilson, 1990. 1 hardbound volume with 4 annual supplements.
Includes all forms.

Juniorplots 3: A Book Talk Guide for Readers Ages 12–16. New York: R. R. Bowker, 1987.
Volumes 1 and 2 are available. Includes narration primarily.

Karp, Rashelle S., and June H. Schlessinger. *Plays for Children and Young Adults: An Evaluative Index and Guide.* New York: Garland, 1991.
Includes narration and drama.

Kennedy, DayAnn, and Mary Ann Vanderwerf. *Science and Technology in Fact and Fiction: A Guide to Children's Books.* New York: R. R. Bowker, 1990.
Includes all forms.

Kennedy, DayAnn, Stella S. Spangler, and Mary Ann Vanderwerf. *Science and Technology in Fact and Fiction: A Guide to Young Adult Books.* New York: R. R. Bowker, 1990.
Includes all forms.

Kennemer, Phyllis K. *Using Literature to Teach Middle Grades about War.* Phoenix, AZ: Oryx Press, 1992.
Includes narration primarily.

Kies, Cosette. *Supernatural Fiction for Teens: More Than 1300 Good Paperbacks to Read for Wonderment, Fear, and Fun.* Littleton, CO: Libraries Unlimited, 1992.
Includes narration primarily.

Kister, Kenneth F. *Kister's Best Dictionaries for Adults and Young People: A Comparative Guide.* Phoenix, AZ: Oryx Press, 1992.

———. *Kister's Best Encyclopedias: A Guide to General and Specialized Encyclopedias.* Phoenix, AZ: Oryx Press, 1994.
Includes exposition primarily.

Kuipers, Barbara J. *American Indian Reference Books for Children and Young Adults.* Littleton, CO: Libraries Unlimited, 1991.
Includes exposition and narration primarily.

Landers Film Review. Escondido, CA: Landers Associates, 1960-present. Quarterly.
Includes all forms.

Lankford, Mary D. *Films for Learning, Thinking and Doing.* Littleton, CO: Libraries Unlimited, 1990.
Includes all forms.

Lenz, Millicent. *Nuclear Age Literature for Youth: The Quest for a Life-Affirming Ethic.* Chicago: American Library Association, 1990.
Includes all forms.

Li, Marjorie H., and Peter Li. *Understanding Asian Americans: A Curriculum Resource Guide.* New York: Neal-Schuman, 1990.
Includes all forms.

McBride, William G. *High Interest—Easy Reading: A Booklist for Junior and Senior High School Students.* Urbana, IL: National Council of Teachers of English, 1990.
Includes all forms.

Magazines for Young Adults: Selections for School and Public Libraries. Chicago: American Library Association, 1984.
Includes all forms.

Magazines for Young People. New York: R. R. Bowker, 1991.
Includes all forms.

Malinowsky, H. Robert, ed. *Best Science and Technology Reference Books for Young People.* Phoenix, AZ: Oryx Press, 1991.
Includes all forms.

Mathematics Teacher. Reston, VA: National Council of Teachers of Mathematics. 8 issues per year.
Includes exposition and procedural forms primarily.

Media Review Digest. Ann Arbor, MI: Pieran Press. Annual.
Includes all forms.

Multicultural Children's and Young Adult Literature: A Selected Listing of Books Published Between 1980–88. Madison, WI: University of Wisconsin-Madison Press, 1989.
Includes all forms.

Museum of Science and Industry Basic List of Children's Science Books. Chicago: American Library Association. Annual.
Includes all forms.

Myers, Sally L., and Blanche Woolls. *Substance Abuse: A Resource Guide for Secondary Schools*. Littleton, CO: Libraries Unlimited, 1991.
Includes exposition and persuasion.

Nakamura, Joyce. *High Interest Books for Teens*. Detroit: Gale Research, 1988.
Includes all forms.

The Newbery and Caldecott Awards: A Guide to the Medal and Honor Books. Chicago: American Library Association, 1991.
Includes narration primarily.

Nichols, Margaret Irby. *Guide to Reference Books for School Libraries*. Littleton, CO: Libraries Unlimited, 1986.
Includes exposition and procedural forms primarily.

Nothin' but the Best: Best of the Best Books for Young Adults 1966–1986. Chicago: Young Adult Library Services Association/American Library Association, 1986.
Includes narration primarily.

On Cassette: A Comprehensive Bibliography of Spoken Word Audio Cassettes. New York: R. R. Bowker, 1985-present. Annual.
Includes all forms.

Only the Best: The Annual Guide to the Highest-Rated Educational Software; Preschool-Grade 12. New York: R. R. Bowker. Annual.
Includes all forms.

Only the Best: The Cumulative Guide to Highest-Rated Educational Software, 1985–1989. New York: R. R. Bowker, 1989.
Includes all forms.

Ott, Bill. *Booklist's Guide to the Year's Best Books*. Detroit: Gale Research, 1992.
Includes all forms.

Outstanding Biographies for the College Bound. Chicago: Young Adult Library Services Association/American Library Association, 1991.
Includes narration primarily with emphasis on biography.

Outstanding Books for the "Current Scene" for the College Bound. Chicago: Young Adult Library Services Association/American Library Association, 1991.
Includes all forms.

Outstanding Fiction for the College Bound. Chicago: Young Adult Library Services Association/American Library Association, 1991.
Includes narration primarily.

Outstanding Non-Fiction for the College Bound. Chicago: Young Adult Library Services Association/American Library Association, 1991.
Includes exposition primarily.

Outstanding Science Trade Books for Children. Arlington, VA: National Science Teachers Association. Annual, in March issue of *Science and Children*.
Includes exposition primarily.

Outstanding Theater for the College Bound. Chicago: Young Adult Library Services Association/American Library Association, 1991.
Includes narration and drama.

Pellowski, Anne. *World of Storytelling.* New York: H. W. Wilson, 1990.
Includes narration.

Petersen, Carolyn Sue, and Ann D. Fenton. *Reference Books for Children.* Metuchen, NJ: Scarecrow Press, 1992.
Includes all forms with emphasis on exposition.

Pilla, Marianne Laino. *The Best: High/Low Books for Reluctant Readers.* Littleton, CO: Libraries Unlimited, 1990.
Includes all forms.

Poetry Anthologies for Children and Young People. Chicago: American Library Association, 1985.
Includes narration and description.

Portraying the Disabled: A Guide to Nonfiction. New York: R. R. Bowker, 1991.
Includes exposition and procedural forms.

Quick Picks for Great Reading. Chicago: Young Adult Library Services Association/American Library Association, 1991.
Includes narration primarily.

Reed, Arethea. *Comics to Classics: A Parent's Guide to Books for Teens and Preteens.* Newark, DE: International Reading Association, 1988.
Includes narration primarily.

Reese, Lyn, and Jean Wilkinson. *Women in the World: Annotated History Resources for the Secondary Student.* Metuchen, NJ: Scarecrow Press, 1987.
Includes narration and exposition.

Reference Sources for Small and Medium-Sized Libraries. Chicago: American Library Association, 1992.
Includes exposition primarily.

Richardson, Selma K. *Magazines for Children: A Guide for Parents, Teachers, and Librarians.* Chicago: American Library Association, 1991.
Includes all forms.

Robertson, Debra. *Portraying Persons with Disabilities: An Annotated Bibliography of Fiction for Children and Teenagers.* New York: R. R. Bowker, 1992.
Includes narration.

Rochman, Hazel. *Against Borders: Promoting Books for a Multicultural World.* Chicago: American Library Association, 1993.
Includes narration primarily.

———. *Tales of Love and Terror: Booktalking the Classics, Old and New.* Chicago: American Library Association, 1987.
Includes narration primarily.

Rosenberg, Betty, and Diana Tixier Herald. *Genreflecting: A Guide to Reading Interests in Genre Fiction.* Littleton, CO: Libraries Unlimited, 1992.
Includes narration primarily with emphasis on the novel.

Rosenberg, Judith K., and C. Allen Nichols. *Young People's Books in Series.* Littleton, CO: Libraries Unlimited, 1992.
Includes all forms.

Rudman, Masha K., Kathleen Dunne Gagne, and Joanne E. Bernstein. *Books to Help Children Cope with Separation and Loss: An Annotated Bibliography, Vol. 4*. New York: R. R. Bowker, 1993.
  Includes all forms.

Schon, Isabel. *Books in Spanish for Children and Young Adults: An Annotated Guide. Series III*. Metuchen, NJ: Scarecrow Press, 1985.
  Series I and II are also available. Includes narration primarily.

————. *Books in Spanish for Children and Young Adults: An Annotated Guide. Series V*. Metuchen, NJ: Scarecrow Press, 1987.
  Includes narration primarily.

————. *Books in Spanish for Children and Young Adults: An Annotated Guide. Series V*. Metuchen, NJ: Scarecrow Press, 1989.
  Includes narration primarily.

————. *Books in Spanish for Children and Young Adults: An Annotated Guide. Series VI*. Metuchen, NJ: Scarecrow Press, 1993.
  Includes narration primarily.

School Library Journal. New York: R. R. Bowker. Monthly.
  Includes all forms.

School Library Media Quarterly. Chicago: American Association of School Librarians/American Library Association. Quarterly.

Schwann Record and Tape Guide. New York: ABC Publications, 1986-present. Quarterly.
  Includes all forms.

Science Books and Films. Washington DC: American Association for the Advancement of Science. 5 issues per year.
  Includes all forms with emphasis on exposition.

Science Fair Project Index, 1981–1984. Metuchen, NJ: Scarecrow Press, 1986.
  Earlier edition is also available. Includes procedural forms.

The Science Teacher. Arlington, VA: National Science Teachers Association. 9 issues per year.
  Includes exposition and procedural forms primarily.

Selecting Materials for and about Hispanic and East Asian Children and Young People. Hamden, CT: Shoestring Press, 1986.
  Includes all forms.

Senior High School Catalog. New York: H. W. Wilson, 1992. 1 hardbound with 4 annual supplements.
  Includes all forms.

Shaevel, Evelyn, Peggy O'Donnell, Susan Goldberg, and Rolly Kent. *Courtly Love in the Shopping Mall: Humanities Programming for Young Adults*. Chicago: American Library Association, 1991.
  Includes narration primarily with emphasis on the novel.

Shapiro, Lillian L., and Barbara Stein. *Fiction for Youth: A Guide to Recommended Books*. New York: Neal-Schuman, 1992.
  Includes narration.

Sheehy, Eugene Paul. *Guide to Reference Books.* Chicago: American Library Association, 1986.
Includes exposition primarily.

Sheilds, Nancy E. *Index to Literary Criticism for Young Adults.* Metuchen, NJ: Scarecrow Press, 1988.
Includes all forms.

Social Education. Washington, DC: National Council for the Social Studies. 7 issues per year.
Includes all forms.

The Software Encyclopedia. New York: R. R. Bowker. Annual.
Includes all forms.

Spencer, Pam. *What Do Young Adults Read Next?* Detroit: Gale Research, 1993.
Includes narration primarily.

Sprit, Diana L. *Introducing More Books: A Guide for Middle Grades.* New York: R. R. Bowker, 1978.
Includes narration primarily.

Sprug, Joseph W. *Index to Fairy Tales, 1987–1992, Including 310 Collections of Fairy Tales, Folktales, Myths, and Legends with Significant Pre-1987 Titles Not Previously Indexed.* Metuchen, NJ: Scarecrow Press, 1994.
Includes narration with emphasis on myth, folktale, legend, and fable.

Stanton, Greta W. *Children of Separation: An Annotated Bibliography for Professionals.* Metuchen, NJ: Scarecrow Press, 1994.
Includes all forms.

Storytelling Magazine. Jonesboro, TN: National Association for the Preservation and Perpetuation of Storytelling. Quarterly.
Includes narration.

Strickland, Charlene. *Dogs, Cats, and Horses: A Resource Guide to the Literature for Young People.* Littleton, CO: Libraries Unlimited, 1990.
Includes all forms.

Teens' Favorite Books: Young Adults' Choices 1987–1992. Newark, DE: International Reading Association, 1992.
Includes narration primarily.

Topical Reference Books. New York: R. R. Bowker, 1991.
Includes exposition primarily.

Totten, Herman L., and Rita W. Brown. *Culturally Diverse Library Collections for Youth.* New York: Neal-Schuman, 1993.
Includes all forms.

United States History: A Resource for Secondary Schools, Vol. 1 and 2. Santa Barbara, CA: ABC-CLIO, 1989.
Includes all forms.

University Press Books for Secondary School Libraries. Chicago: American Library Association, 1968-present. Annual.
Includes all forms.

VanMeter, Vandelia. *American History for Children and Young Adults: An Annotated Bibliographic Index.* Littleton, CO: Libraries Unlimited, 1990.
Includes exposition and narration primarily.

————. *World History for Children and Young Adults: An Annotated Bibliographic Index.* Littleton, CO: Libraries Unlimited, 1992.
Includes narration and exposition.

Venturing into Cultures: A Resource Book of Multicultural Materials and Programs. Chicago: American Library Association, 1991.
Includes all forms.

Vertical File Index: A Subject and Title Index to Selected Pamphlet Materials. New York: H. W. Wilson. 11 issues per year.
Includes exposition, persuasion, and procedural forms primarily.

The Video Source Book. Detroit: Gale Research. Annual.
Includes all forms.

VOYA (Voice of Youth Advocates). Metuchen, NJ: Scarecrow Press, 1978-present. Bimonthly.
Includes all forms.

Walker, Elinor. *Book Bait: Detailed Notes on Adult Books Popular with Young Adults.* Chicago: American Library Association, 1988.
Includes narration primarily.

Walter, Virginia A. *War and Peace Literature for Children and Young Adults: A Resource Guide to Significant Issues.* Phoenix, AZ: Oryx Press, 1993.
Includes narration and exposition primarily.

Wear, Terri A. *The Horse's Name Was . . . A Dictionary of Famous Horses from History, Literature, Mythology, Television and Movies.* Metuchen, NJ: Scarecrow Press, 1987.
Includes all forms.

Webb, C. Anne. *Your Reading: A Booklist for Junior High and Middle School Students.* Urbana, IL: National Council of Teachers of English, 1993.
Includes all forms.

Welton, Ann. *Explorers and Exploration: The Best Resources for Grades 5 through 9.* Phoenix, AZ: Oryx Press, 1993.
Includes all forms.

Whiteley, Sandy. *Dictionaries for Adults and Children.* Chicago: American Library Association, 1991.
Includes exposition.

Wilkin, Binnie Tate. *Survival Themes in Fiction for Children and Young People.* Metuchen, NJ: Scarecrow Press, 1993.
Includes narration.

Williams, Helen E. *Books by African-American Authors and Illustrators for Children and Young Adults.* Chicago: American Library Association, 1991.
Includes narration primarily.

Wilson Library Bulletin. New York: H. W. Wilson, 1939-present. 10 issues per year.
Includes all forms.

Wurth, Shirley. *Books for You: A Booklist for Senior High Students.* Urbana, IL: National Council of Teachers of English, 1992.
Includes narration primarily.

Young Adult Reader's Advisor. New York: R. R. Bowker, 1992.
  Includes all forms.
Young Adults' Choices. Newark, DE: International Reading Association. Annual.
  Includes all forms.
Zvirin, Stephanie. *The Best Years of Their Lives: A Resource Guide for Teenagers in Crisis.* Chicago: American Library Association, 1992.
  Includes all forms with an emphasis on narration and exposition.

MASTER WEB OF LITERARY FORMS APPROACHES

In summary, a literary forms approach is useful for teaching students about literary structures and for introducing common forms throughout the world. Such an approach helps students develop reading skills and become more confident in deciding which forms are most appropriate for meeting their needs. Young people may decide on forms that give them comfort or pleasure. For teachers or library media specialists, a literary forms approach is easy to implement and enables them to draw from a plethora of subjects to appeal to a wide reading audience.

The forms generally group themselves in subgroups around major forms of writing, primarily categorized by message, purpose, or intent. Narrative forms include the traditional forms that have originated from an oral storytelling past. Examples include fables, folktales, myths, legends, epics, ballads, and rhymes. More modern forms of narration include autobiography, biography, diary or journal, story poem, novel, and short story. The dramatic form comprises plays, skits, monologues and dialogues, and musical dramas or operas. Exposition includes articles in newspapers and magazines, pamphlets and textual materials, reports, essays, and letters. Speeches, sermons, informal arguments, debates, and advertisements are types of persuasive writing. Examples of procedural writing may be found in recipes, directions, instructions, and experiments. Finally, descriptive writing, when not combined with other forms, includes travelogues, catalog descriptions, and descriptive poetry.

The following master web of literary forms approaches (Figure 1) shows the relationships of the major forms and subforms. Subforms will be defined in individual chapters.

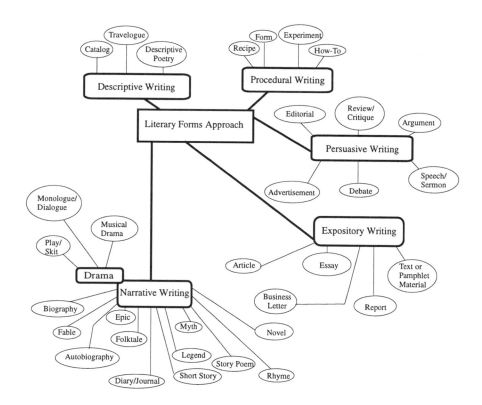

Figure 1. Master Web of Literary Forms Approaches

2

Narrative Writing

INTRODUCTION

"Tell me a story." This age-old request precedes the beginning of an ancient form of entertainment and instruction. The literary form narration captures a sequence of actions that occur in a given setting and lead to a climax and to the resolution of a conflict. The setting and time frame may or may not be familiar to the reader, but it must establish a structure in which the reader can visualize the events. While the characters involved in the action may be loved or hated, they must be compelling to the reader, who identifies with them in order to experience the action vicariously. The point of view expressed may or may not be that of the author. The author's style encompasses vocabulary, word order, figurative language, syntax, sentence structure, and other devices.

Readers of narrative writing know that they can expect a sequence of events that leads to a climax and a conclusion, and they learn to identify types of endings that may be satisfying to them. It is difficult to pinpoint what motivates students to read another story, but the need to share in others' stories and to tell one's own is powerful. A narrative approach capitalizes on the students' need to read about events in the context of place and time and on their memory of strong characters with whom they can identify.

Narrative writing has been studied in many disciplines, from psychology and history to education and linguistics. There are many possible approaches to narrative. One approach is through character. From their first experiences with basal readers to their encounters with lengthy novels, readers expect that characters will be introduced at the beginning of a story. If these characters engage the reader, the reading experience is pursued through a series of events to the climax. Readers usually hope that the ending is a satisfying one. After all, time has been invested in getting to know the characters. Readers express satisfaction with a story's ending because they identify with the characters and would have wanted the same conclusion for themselves, or because the situation in which the character found himself or herself warranted the ending. Whatever the reason, the reader was able to enjoy the suspension of his or her own life for a time to become involved vicariously in another experience of life.

Professional Sources

The following list includes several sources for studying text as narrative, including the elements of narrative form such as plot, characterization, setting, point of view, tone, mood, and style. A search of library catalogs and databases using key words such as *narrative text, narrative study, style,* and *plot* will provide even more information.

General

Adams, Jeff. *The Conspiracy of Text: The Place of Narrative in the Development of Thought.* New York: Routledge and Kegan Paul, 1986.

Banfield, Ann. *Unspeakable Sentences: Narration and Representation in the Language of Fiction.* New York: Routledge and Kegan Paul, 1982.

Black, Elizabeth. "The Nature of Fictional Discourse: A Case Study." *Applied Linguistics* 10, no. 3 (September 1989), pp. 281-93.

Britton, Bruce K. *The Narrative Thought and Narrative Language.* Hillsdale, NJ: Erlbaum, 1990.

Caws, Mary Ann. *Reading Frames in Modern Fiction.* Princeton, NJ: Princeton University Press, 1985.

Chafe, Wallace L. *The Pear Stories: Cognitive, Cultural, and Linguistic Aspects of Narrative Production.* Norwood, NJ: Ablex Pub. Corp., 1980.

Coste, Didier. *Narrative as Communication.* Minneapolis, MN: University of Minnesota Press, 1989.

Cummings, Melodie. *Literature Line-Up: A Study of Different Forms of Literature for Intermediate Grade Children.* Cedar Falls, IA: Area Education Agency 7, 1980. ED 239205.

Dry, Helen Aristar. "Approaches to Coherence in Natural and Literary Narrative," in *Text Connexity, Text Coherence: Aspects, Methods, Results,* ed. Emel Sozer (Hamburg: Buske, 1985).

Fleischman, Suzanne. *Tense and Narrativity: From Medieval Performance to Modern Fiction*. Austin, TX: University of Texas Press, 1990.

Genette, Grard. *Narrative Discourse: An Essay in Method*. Ithaca, NY: Cornell University Press, 1980.

Greimas, Algirdas Julien. *On Meaning: Selected Writings in Semiotic Theory*. Minneapolis, MN: University of Minnesota Press, 1987.

Hardee, A. Maynor. *Narratology and Narrative*. Columbia, SC: University of South Carolina Press, 1990.

Harris, John, and Jeff Wilkinson. *Reading Children's Writing: A Linguistic View*. Boston: Allen and Unwin, 1986.

Jones, Denis. *The Matrix of Narrative: Family Systems and the Semiotics of Story*. Hawthorn, NY: Mouton de Gruyter, 1990.

Kitzhaber, Albert R. *The Narrative Mode: Literature Curriculum V. Teacher Version*. Eugene, OR: University of Oregon Press. ED 015906.

Leitch, Thomas M. *What Stories Are: Narrative Theory and Interpretation*. University Park, PA: Pennsylvania State University Press, 1986.

Mellard, James M. *Doing Tropology: Analysis of Narrative Discourse*. Champaign, IL: University of Illinois Press, 1987.

Morrow, Daniel G. "Prepositions and Verb Aspect in Narrative Understanding." *Journal of Memory and Language* 24, no. 4 (August 1985), pp. 390-404.

Nicholson, Tom, and David Hill. "Good Readers Don't Guess: Taking Another Look at the Issue of Whether Children Read Words Better in Context or in Isolation." *Reading Psychology: An International Quarterly* 6, nos. 3-4 (1985), pp. 181-98.

Omanson, Richard C. "An Analysis of Narratives: Identifying Central, Supportive, and Distracting Content." *Discourse Processes: A Multidisciplinary Journal* 5, nos. 3-4 (July-December 1982), pp. 195-224.

Peterson, Carole, and Allyssa McCabe. *Developmental Psycholinguistics: Three Ways of Looking at a Child's Narrative*. New York: Plenum Press, 1983.

Pinto, Julio C. M. *The Reading of Time: A Semantic-Semiotic Approach*. Hawthorn, NY: Mouton de Gruyter, 1989.

Polkinghorne, Donald. *Narrative Knowing and the Human Sciences*. Albany, NY: State University of New York Press, 1988.

Prince, Gerald. *Narratology: The Form and Functioning of Narrative*. Hawthorn, NY: Mouton de Gruyter, 1982.

Salazar, Sandra Brauner. *Prediction/Fulfillment Application in a Frame-Based Story Comprehension System*. College Park, MD: University of Maryland Press, 1977.

Shuman, Amy. *Storytelling Rights: The Uses of Oral and Written Texts by Urban Adolescents*. New York: Cambridge University Press, 1986.

Stibbs, Andrew. *Reading Narrative as Literature: Signs of Life*. Philadelphia: Open University Press, 1991.

Toolan, Michal J. *Narrative: A Critical Linguistic Introduction*. New York: Routledge, 1988.

Wanner, Susan V. *On with the Story: Adolescents Learning through Narrative.* Portsmouth, NH: Boynton/Cook, 1994.

Wolf, Yuval, Joel Walter, and Susan Holzman. "Integration of Semantic and Structural Constraints in Narrative Comprehension." *Discourse Processes: A Multidisciplinary Journal* 12, no. 2 (April-June 1989), pp. 149-67.

Young, Katharine Galloway. *Taleworlds and Storyrealms: The Phenomenology of Narrative.* Hingham, MA: Nijhoff/Kluwer Academic Publishers, 1987.

Elements of Narrative

Dionisio, Marie. "Responding to Literary Elements through Mini-Lessons and Dialogue Journals." *English Journal* 80, no. 1 (January 1991): 40-44.

Keller, Rodney D. "Movies and Literary Elements." *Teaching English in the Two-Year College* 14, no. 4 (December 1987): 273-80.

Literature for Children. Series 9. Verdugo City, CA: Pied Piper Productions, 1984. 5 sound filmstrips: *Plot, Setting, Character, Theme,* and *Style.*

Lukens, Rebecca J. *A Critical Handbook of Children's Literature.* Glenview, IL: Scott, Foresman, 1986.

Olsen, Stein Haugom. *The Structure of Literary Understanding.* London: Cambridge University Press, 1978.

Triplett, DeWayne. *The Mapping of Literary Elements by Eighth Graders and College Sophomores Following the Reading of a Narrative.* Paper presented at the annual meeting of the National Reading Conference, Dallas, TX, December 2-5, 1981. ED 227467.

Weiss, Adele B. "Using Picture Storybooks to Teach Literary Elements to the Disabled Reader." *Pointer* 27, no. 1 (Fall 1982), pp. 8-10.

Wellek, Ren, and Austin Warren. *Theory of Literature.* New York: Harcourt Brace Jovanovich, 1977.

Plot

Balasa, Michael A. "Increasing Reading Comprehension by Teaching Plot Complexity." *Reading Improvement* 14, no. 1 (Spring 1977), pp. 48-51.

Block, Lawrence. *Writing the Novel from Plot to Print.* Cincinnati, OH: Writers Digest Books, 1979.

Brittain, Bill. "The Plotting of 'Mr. Dredd.'" *New Advocate* 1, no. 2 (Spring 1988), pp. 84-91.

Brooks, Peter. *Reading for the Plot: Design and Intention in Narrative.* New York: Knopf, 1984.

Caserio, Robert L. *Plot, Story, and the Novel: From Dickens and Poe to the Modern Period.* Princeton, NJ: Princeton University Press, 1979.

Copeland, Jeffrey S. "Multiple-Storyline Books for Young Adults: Why?" *English Journal* 76, no. 8 (December 1987), 52-54.

Dibell, Ansen. *Plot.* Cincinnati, OH: Writer's Digest Books, 1988.

Graesser, Arthur C., et al. "Answers to Why-Questions Expose the Organization of Story Plot and Predict Recall of Actions." *Journal of Verbal Learning and Verbal Behavior* 19, no. 1 (February 1980), pp. 110-19.

Harris, William Foster. *The Basic Patterns of Plot.* Norman, OK: University of Oklahoma Press, 1959.

Hawkes, Peter. "Teaching Plot." *Exercise Exchange* 33, no. 2 (Spring 1988): pp. 36-38.

Jose, Paul E. "Liking of Plan-Based Stories: The Role of Goal Importance and Goal Attainment Difficulty." *Discourse Processes* 11, no. 3 (July-September 1988), pp. 261-73.

Kinney, Maretha A., and John Schmidt. *Relating the Parts to the Whole in Novel Reading: Using Story Grammars to Teach Plot Development in Novels.* Paper presented at the annual meeting of the International Reading Association, Philadelphia, PA, April 13-17, 1986. ED 276990.

Lehnert, Wendy G., and Cynthia Loiselle. "An Introduction to Plot Units," in *Semantic Structures: Advances in Natural Language Processing*, ed. David L. Waltz. Hillsdale, NJ: Erlbaum, 1989.

Noble, June, and William Noble. *Steal This Plot: A Writer's Guide to Story Structure and Plagiarism.* Middlebury, VT: P. S. Ericksson, 1985.

Norton, Donna E. "Understanding Plot Structures (Engaging Children in Literature)." *Reading Teacher* 46, no. 3 (November 1992), pp. 254-58.

Phelan, James. *Reading People, Reading Plots: Character, Progression, and the Interpretation of Narrative.* Chicago: University of Chicago Press, 1989.

Phillips, Henry Albert. *The Plot of the Short Story: An Exhaustive Study, Both Synthetical and Analytical, with Copious Examples, Making the Work a Practical Treatise (Rev. to Include a Syllabus for Teachers).* Folcroft, PA: Folcroft Library Editions, 1974.

———. *The Universal Plot: An Examination of the Elements of Plot Material and Construction, Combined with a Complete Index and a Progressive Category in Which the Source, Life and End of All Dramatic Conflict and Plot Matter Are Classified, Making the Work a Practical Treatise.* Folcroft, PA: Folcroft Library Editions, 1973.

Prentice, Penelope. *Tell Me a Story I'll Never Forget or Deconstructing Traditional Narrative Plot/Myths to Challenge the Ethics of Conflict.* Paper presented at the annual meeting of the College English Association, Pittsburgh, PA, March 27-29, 1992. ED 347531.

Prince, Gerald. *A Grammar of Stories: An Introduction.* Hawthorn, NY: Mouton de Gruyter, 1973.

Ragussis, Michael. *Acts of Naming: The Family Plot in Fiction.* New York: Oxford University Press, 1986.

Reiser, Brian, et al. "Thematic Knowledge Structures in the Understanding and Generation of Narratives." *Discourse Processes* 8, no. 3 (July-September 1985), pp. 357-89.

Rockwell, F. A. *How to Write Plots That Sell.* Chicago: Contemporary Books, 1975.

Rose, Brian. "Thickening the Plot." *Journal of Communication* 29, no. 4 (Fall 1979), pp. 81-84.

The Story's Blueprint: Plot and Structure in Short Fiction. S. Burlington, VT: Maryland Public Television/Annenberg/CPB Project, 1992. 52 min. 1 videocassette.

Sudol, David. "Creating and Killing Stanley Realbozo, or Teaching Characterization and Plot in English 10." *English Journal* 72, no. 6 (October 1983), pp. 63-66.

Tilley, E. Allen. "The Modes of Fiction: A Plot Morphology." *College English* 39, no. 6 (February 1978): pp. 692-706.

———. *Plot Snakes and the Dynamics of Narrative Experience.* Gainesville, FL: University of Florida Press, 1992.

Setting

Fisher, Philip. *Hard Facts: Setting and Form in the American Novel.* New York: Oxford University Press, 1985.

Hartman, Donald K., and Jerome Drost. *Themes and Settings in Fiction: A Bibliography of Bibliographies.* Westport, CT: Greenwood Press, 1988.

Kelly, Joanne. *On Location: Settings from Famous Children's Books #1.* Englewood, CO: Libraries Unlimited, 1992.

Lutwack, Leonard. *The Role of Place in Literature.* Syracuse, NY: Syracuse University Press, 1984.

Noble, William. *Make That Scene: A Writer's Guide to Setting, Mood, and Atmosphere.* Middlebury, VT: P. S. Eriksson, 1988.

Characterization

Card, Orson Scott. *Characters and Viewpoint.* Cincinnati, OH: Writer's Digest Books, 1988.

Character, Setting, Plot. Northbrook, IL: Anthony Roland Collection of Films on Art/ICA Video, 1989. 21 min. 1 videocassette.

Docherty, Thomas. *Reading (Absent) Character: Towards a Theory of Characterization in Fiction.* New York: Clarendon Press, 1983.

Dreher, Joyce. "Character Contrast." *Reading Teacher* 42, no. 7 (March 1989), pp. 551-552.

Gallo, Donald R. "Writing from Literature." *Exercise Exchange* 27, no. 1 (Fall 1982), pp. 32-34.

Gardiner, Cynthia P. *The Sophoclean Chorus: A Study of Character and Function.* Iowa City, IA: University of Iowa Press, 1987.

Harris, Laurie Lanzen. *Characters in 20th Century Literature.* Detroit: Gale Research, 1990.

Morrow, Daniel G. "Prominent Characters and Events Organize Narrative Understanding." *Journal of Memory and Language* 24, no. 3 (June 1985), pp. 304-319.

Peck, Robert Newton. *Fiction Is Folks: How to Create Unforgettable Characters.* Cincinnati, OH: Writer's Digest Books, 1983.

Price, Martin. *Forms of Life: Character and Moral Imagination in the Novel.* New Haven, CT: Yale University Press, 1983.

Swindon, Patrick. *Unofficial Selves: Character in the Novel from Dickens to the Present Day.* New York: Macmillan, 1973.

Wilson, Mary E. *Representing Children's Book Characters.* Metuchen, NJ: Scarecrow Press, 1989.

Point of View

Folsom, James K. "Teaching Creative Writing Through Point of View." *Journal of English Teaching Techniques* 5, no. 2 (Summer 1972), pp. 1-22.

Kenzel, Elaine, and Jean Williams. *Point of View, Language Arts: 5114.62.* Miami, FL: Dade County Public Schools, 1972. ED 087032.

Noe, Marcia. "Teaching Point of View in the Modern Fiction Class." *Teaching English in the Two-Year College* 14, no. 3 (October 1987), pp. 211-213.

Wilhoit, Stephen. "Moffett and Point of View: A Creative Writing Assignment Sequence." *Journal of Teaching Writing* 5, no. 2 (Fall 1986), pp. 297-305.

Style

Bogdan, Deanne. "A Rhetorical Approach to Teaching Prose Style in Senior High School English." *English Quarterly* 9, nos. 1–2 (Spring Semester 1976), pp. 115-128.

Cooper, Elizabeth J. *Style: Applications for the Student Writer.* Paper presented at the annual meeting of the Canadian Council of Teachers of English, Saskatoon, Canada, August 15-20, 1982. ED 219787.

Gage, John T. "Philosophies of Style and Their Implications for Composition." *College English* 41, no. 6 (February 1980), pp. 615-622.

Gaston, Thomas E. "Teaching a Concept of Style for Literature and Composition." *English Journal* 59, no. 1 (January 1970), pp. 65-70, 98.

Hiatt, Mary P. *Speaking of Style: How Objective Can One Be?* Paper presented at the annual meeting of the Conference on College Composition and Communication, Minneapolis, Minnesota, April 5-7, 1979. ED 175000.

Jolly, Peggy. "A Question of Style." *Exercise Exchange* 26. no. 2 (Spring 1982), pp. 39-40. ED 236601.

Pringle, Ian. "Why Teach Style? A Review-Essay." *College Composition and Communication* 34, no. 1 (February 1983), pp. 91-98.

Rankin, Elizabeth D. "Revitalizing Style: Toward a New Theory and Pedagogy." *Freshman English News* 14, no. 1 (Spring 1985), pp. 8-13.

Vonnegut, Kurt. *How To Write with Style. Power of the Printed Word.* New York: International Paper Company, 1980. ED 236589

Zahlan, Anne Ricketson. *Teaching Style through Literature.* Paper presented at the annual meeting of the Conference on College Composition and Communication, New Orleans, LA, March 13-15, 1986. ED 271787.

TRADITIONAL NARRATIVE FORMS

Narrative forms have developed over time (Figure 2). Prior to written narrative was spoken narrative. Traditional forms of narrative include myths, legends, fables, folktales, ballads, and epics. These traditional forms began with the storyteller. Each form served a specific function within the lives of its tellers and listeners. In early times, various peoples are believed to have developed myths that helped explain the religious beliefs significant to the life of the group. Some were creation myths that helped people understand their beginnings and helped explain natural processes. Folktales were separate from myths. They were secular stories often told for amusement. Legends were entertaining, but more than that, they were used to instruct, telling of individuals, who in some way embodied the ideal characteristics of the group. Often legends also included significant historical events from the groups' past. They were many times saved in the form of epic poetry, which could have assisted the group in remembering the stories. Rhymes and jokes may also have been part of this tradition. Finally, parables and fables were intended to instruct and served as a medium for passing along moral or ethical values held by the group. The drama as play, musical drama, dialog, and chorus also grew out of this tradition.

As peoples developed sophisticated writing, literary forms were created to meet other needs. The narrative can be seen in modern written forms such as the autobiography, biography, diaries and journals, story poems, novels, short stories, and the ubiquitous anecdotes and short narratives found in basal readers. When modern forms are related in purpose to older, more traditional forms, similarities are at once evident. For example, autobiographies, biographies, diaries, and journals relate to legend in that the forms focus on individuals and the events of their lives. However, each of these forms differs in focus and point of view. By definition, a biography is the story of a person's life written by an individual other than the subject of the story. The point of view changes in an autobiography because the person writes his or her own story. The focus of biographies and autobiographies is on relating past events in the lives of real individuals. Diaries and journals are also very personal in nature; they are firsthand accounts of the events in the lives of individuals. In the case of such documents, experiences and thoughts of an individual are recorded daily or regularly and are often not meant to be read by others.

Novels are related to the folktale in that they are often meant to entertain. Novels are fairly complicated stories that rely on lengthy and intricate sequences. They allow the reader to escape, provide adventure, and offer ideas about problems. Characters are well developed and tend to engage the reader in personal identification with them. Short stories are, of course, shorter than novels and can often be read in one sitting. Short stories have proliferated in the twentieth century but are hardly new. If one looks at short stories and compares them in length to parables or fables, some similarities may be seen. One might view the story poem as similar to the epic, though often without the same grand reason for being.

Figure 2. Narrative Forms

Activities in this lesson will be based on three examples of narrative. The myth is an example of narrative, originally believed to be a way of explaining spiritual beliefs. The fable is an abbreviated way of teaching. Both of these forms are written in third person. Finally, autobiography has been chosen as an example of first person narrative, a more modern written form. Activities for novels, short stories, folktales, biographies, and the other narrative forms may be found in abundance in most current literature curriculum guides.

AUTOBIOGRAPHY

When an individual chooses to write an account of a significant portion of his or her life, the product is an autobiography. Such a literary effort offers the reader insight into the emotions, events, and culture of the author and the society in which he or she lived. There is a small, collected group of autobiographies appropriate for use by children and young adults. These autobiographies can be categorized by several common characteristics.

In all of them, the author writes about his or her own life experiences. The text is usually written in first person and in chronological order. Anecdotes often make up a major part of the work, selected by the author as important to the telling of his or her story. The writer often weaves the anecdotes and descriptions together to create a dominant impression of himself or herself. Thus, the author provides the reader with "truth" about the author as he or she sees it. In most autobiographies, the author's point of view can be clearly determined. Often, in works for children or young adults, the purpose is to share some insight that will make the reader's life better.

For this reason, autobiographies that might be motivating to young adults cannot appear "preachy." The individual should have some appeal, and that appeal should be apparent. The following criteria may be helpful for selecting works:

1. Purpose (Does the author have an identifiable point in mind, and was this accomplished in the work? Does the author tell his or her story for an identifiable audience?)
2. Author (For what major contribution is the author known? Can the author's philosophy of life be recognized in the work?)
3. Authenticity (Does the author present his or her story as factually or accurately as possible? Do the author's facts match accurately the history of the time in which he or she is writing? How does the author present his or her contribution? How does the author present the obstacles which had to be overcome?)
4. Appropriateness (What is the instructional level of the author's work in terms of vocabulary, concepts, logical sequence, illustrations, literary quality, and readability? Are controversial issues presented by the

author recognizable? Does the author avoid overuse of emotionalism? How does the author's presentation of himself or herself compare with other presentations? What has the author chosen to emphasize? What about the story will be interesting to students?)

5. Content (How extensive is the author's coverage of his or her life? How does information presented by the author differ from other sources? Is the content clear?)

6. Technical quality of the presentation (Is the material physically appealing? Is the work well written?)

7. Supporting opinion (Has the author's work been reviewed in other sources?)

The criteria for selection of autobiographies are useful in making some decisions about the writing. Young adults may be motivated to read about an individual for many reasons. Sometimes a person is "sensational." Other times the individual is admirable for some reason. Perhaps the individual has succeeded at an endeavor for which a young person has ambitions. Perhaps the individual embodies "good" qualities a child would like to emulate, or less desirable qualities the child wants to avoid.

It is interesting to note that autobiographies popular with and written for young adults tend to fall into categories with similar purposes. People who have had to overcome great obstacles wish to share their triumphs and often do so in autobiographies. In the past 20 years prominent obstacles that have been overcome include racial prejudice, physical handicaps, sex-role stereotyping, competition, and survival in times of war. Authors find autobiography a powerful means of sharing the experience of overcoming problems. Another group of autobiographical narratives deals with childhood remembrances or memories of more pleasant times. Because autobiographies fall so easily into categories, it is possible to prepare motivational book talks or units of instruction tailored to particular interests of students.

Autobiographical Categories

1. Adventure and Struggle (Individuals struggle against nature or strive to excel in their field of endeavor)

2. Handicaps (Individuals cope with their handicaps and manage to succeed in spite of them)

3. The Minority Experience (Individuals excel or learn to cope in spite of the difficulties imposed by racial, sexual, religious, or age prejudice)

4. Memories of Childhood and Life Expectations (Individuals remember significant or pleasant events from childhood or early life that contributed to making them what they have become, or they want to confess some negative aspect of their childhood in the hope that others might learn from their experience)
5. Sports (Individuals excel at physical endeavors)
6. World War II or War (Individuals must cope with the pains and trials of war)

The autobiography, by its nature and purpose, provides a number of worthwhile objectives for the teacher, library media specialist, or parent. Because the author is shaping the text by his or her own memories and need for expression of self-image, the reader often must find a way to identify with the expressed point of view. The author's values and beliefs are exposed in the choice and presentation of anecdotes. The use of first person creates an intimate tone that helps to establish a relationship between the author and the reader. Pronouns and referents relate to the author's personal experience. Depending on the author's background, colloquial expressions and regional slang are sometimes used. The writing is often full of anecdotes retold in a chronological order or with flashbacks to relate to a particular point in a time line underlying the story. Such writing allows the reader to vicariously experience the author's life. If there is something about the author's career or accomplishments that appeals to a young reader, that reader may feel motivated to search for answers, insight, or secrets from the individual.

Professional Sources

Many materials are available to the teacher or library media specialist who wishes to teach about autobiography. The resources recommended are divided into two categories: bibliography or reference works and teaching aids.

Bibliographies and Reference Books

Braxton, Joanne M. *Black Women Writing Autobiography: A Tradition within a Tradition.* Philadelphia: Temple University Press, 1989.

Briscoe, Mary Louise, Barbara Tibias, and Lynn Z. Bloom. *American Autobiography 1945-1980: A Bibliography.* Madison, WI: University of Wisconsin Press, 1982.

Contemporary Authors Autobiography Series. Vol. 1. Detroit: Gale Research, 1984.

Jelinek, Estelle C. *The Tradition of Women's Autobiography: From Antiquity to Present.* New York: Twayne Publishers, 1986.

Kaplan, Louis, James Tyler Cook, Clinton E. Colby, Jr., and Daniel C. Haskell. *A Bibliography of American Autobiographies.* Madison, WI: The University of Wisconsin Press, 1962.

Lilliard, Richard G. *American Life in Autobiography: A Descriptive Guide.* Stanford, CA: Stanford University Press, 1956.

Something About the Author. Autobiography Series. Vol 1-. Detroit: Gale Research, 1986-.

Teaching Aids

Beach, Richard. "Difference in Autobiographical Narratives of English Teachers, College Freshmen, and Seventh Graders." *College Composition and Communication* 38, no. 1 (February 1987), pp. 56-69.

Bloom, Lynn Z. *Autobiography and Audience.* Paper presented at the annual meeting of the Conference on College Composition and Communication, Detroit, MI, March 17-19, 1983. ED 229786.

————. *Recreating Creators: Teaching Students to Edit Autobiographical Materials.* Paper presented at the nnual meeting of the Conference on College Composition and Communication, San Francisco, CA, March 18-20, 1982. ED 219748.

Cohen, Michael. "An Autobiographical Exercise." *Exercise Exchange* 32, no. 1 (Fall 1986), pp. 23-25.

Fleming, Margaret, and Jo McGinnis, eds. *Portraits: Biography and Autobiography in the Secondary School.* Urbana, IL: National Council of Teachers of English, 1985.

Forms of Literature: Biography/Autobiography. Mt. Kisco, NY: Guidance Associates, 1974. 2 sound filmstrips.

Graham, Robert J. *Reading and Writing Self: Autobiography in Education and the Curriculum.* New York: Teachers College Press, 1991.

Kitzhaber, Albert R. *Julius Caesar. Plutarch's Lives. Autobiography. Literature Curriculum IV, Teacher Version.* Eugene, OR: University of Oregon Press. ED 010818.

Mungo, Raymond. *Your Autobiography: More Than 300 Questions to Help You Write Your Personal History.* New York: Collier Books, 1994.

Rochman, Hazel. "Autobiography: Heroes and Monsters." *The Horn Book Magazine* 66 (May-June 1990), p. 297.

Schiff, Peter. "Autobiography Meets the English Class and Everybody Wins." *English Journal* 62, no. 5 (May 1973), pp. 784-786.

Shackleton, Cheryl A. "Making a Book: Autobiography." *School Library Journal* 38 (January 1992), p. 42.

Weinberg, Daniel E. "Viewing the Immigrant Experience in America through Fiction and Autobiography With a Select Bibliography." *History Teacher* 9, no. 3 (May 1976), pp. 409-432.

Zancanella, Don. "Autobiographical Writing and the Reading of Literature." *English Journal* 80 (December 1991), p. 11.

Activity: Oral History

This activity uses oral history techniques to help students gather background information about themselves. It should give them some idea about what goes into writing both an autobiography and a biography.

To prepare students to write their own stories, have them first read an autobiography of their choice so that they have a model to follow. Because the students are still very young, they may not feel that they have much to say. Approaching the task from the standpoint of doing oral history will help them overcome their hesitation. Have the students list events in the lives of persons that they read about that seem important to them. Doing this will help them narrow down what they would like to elaborate on in their own autobiographies.

One of several uses can be made of the resources list. Provide a master list of individuals whose works are represented in the collection and allow students to select a person whom they think is interesting. Choose a category, such as sports figures, and share a brief incident from each of the books that relate to this topic before asking students to make their own selection. Encourage students to browse through the bibliographies and books on their own to find one or two titles that are of interest to them. They might make selections based on the names of the individuals listed.

Provide an outline for students to guide them as they collect ideas for their own autobiographies. Let students focus on certain aspects of their lives. Encourage them to be creative in their approach. They can be either serious or humorous in their personal accounts. The outline could include any or all of the following topics:

- Day they were born
- Firsts (words, sentences, foods, hat, ball thrown, solo bicycle ride, etc.)
- School events
- Family or religious events
- Parents, siblings, grandparents, aunts, and uncles
- Positive or negative experiences
- Events recorded on film, video, or in pictures

Suggest to students that listening to others sometimes helps to prod one's own memory about an event. Encourage them to interview family members and other relatives or friends about shared experiences. Having them take notes or tape their interviews would add to the usefulness of this exercise. Suggest also that they think about what questions they want to ask in the interviews and how they want to ask them. A set of questions designed to help students think about their autobiographies can be found in Raymond Mungo's *Your Autobiography* (Collier, 1994).

Sample Note Form:

Event: _____

My Recollection of Event:

_____

_____

_____

Interviewee's Recollection of Same Event:

_____

_____

_____

When the interviews are completed, students are ready to read their notes or listen to the recordings of their interviews and select the stories they like the best. Instruct them to retell the stories in their own words, drawing from their interviews and from their own memories. Suggest to students that they order the stories and events chronologically to develop a more cohesive autobiography. Stories may be completed with computer word processing programs and printed in more than one format.

Student Sources

Most students begin to enjoy the autobiographies during grades eight through twelve. Note that the interest and Fry readability ranges for the books in the following list should be considered a very rough estimate. Certain books may be less appropriate to younger adolescents because of the nature of the lives and the language that authors have chosen to recount the events in their lives. The list contains both recent and older autobiographies, which can be seen by looking at the copyrights. The abbreviations IL and RL stand for "interest level" and "the Fry readability level" respectively.

Aaron, Henry. *Aaron.* New York: Crowell, 1974. IL: 7-9+.

———. *I Had a Hammer.* New York: HarperCollins, 1990-1992. IL: 7-9+.

Abdul-Jabar, Kareem. *Kareem.* New York: Random House, 1990. IL: 6-8; RL: 7.

Addams, Jane. *Twenty Years at Hull-House.* Urbana, IL: University of Illinois Press, 1990. IL: 7-9+.

Agle, Nan Hayden. *My Animals and Me: An Autobiographical Story.* New York: Seabury Press, 1970. IL: 4-7.

Anderson, Marian. *My Lord, What a Morning: An Autobiography.* New York: Viking, 1956. IL: 7-9+.

Anderson, William R. *First Under the North Pole: The Voyage of the "Nautilus."* New York: World Publishers, 1959. IL: 5-7.

———. *Nautilus 90 North.* New York: World Publishers, 1959. IL: 7-9+.

Andrews, William L. *Journeys in New Worlds: Early American Women's Narratives.* Madison, WI: University of Wisconsin Press, 1990. IL: 8-9+.

Antin, Mary. *The Promised Land.* Princeton, NJ: Princeton University Press, 1985. IL: 7-9+.

Ashabranner, Brent. *The Times of My Life: A Memoir.* New York: Cobblehill Books, 1990. IL: 6-9.

Auerbach, Arnold. *Red Auerbach: An Autobiography.* New York: Putnam, 1977. IL: 7-9+.

Bailey, Pearl. *The Raw Pearl.* New York: Harcourt Brace and World, 1968. IL: 7-9+.

Barnum, Phineas Taylor. *Barnum's Own Story: The Autobiography of P. T. Barnum.* New York: Peter Smith, 1972. IL: 7-9+.

———. *Struggles and Triumphs: Or, Forty Years' Recollection of P. T. Barnum.* New York: Penguin Books, 1981. IL: 7-9+.

Bilberg, Rudy. *In the Shadow of the Eagles: From Barnstormer to Alaska Bush Pilot.* Bothell, WA: Alaska Northwest, 1992. IL: 8-9+.

Blegvad, Eric. *Self-Portrait: Erik Blegvad.* New York: Harper and Row, 1979. IL: 5-8; RL: 7.

Bulla, Robert Clyde. *Grain of Wheat: A Writer Begins.* Boston: Godine, 1985. IL: 3-5; RL: 3.

Byars, Betsy. *The Moon and I.* Englewood Cliffs, NJ: Messner, 1991. IL: 4-7; RL: 6.

Campanella, Roy. *It's Good to Be Alive.* Boston: Little, Brown, 1959. IL: 5-8.

Canutt, Yakima. *Stunt Man: The Autobiography of Yakima Canutt.* New York: Walker, 1979. IL: 8-9+.

Cary, Lorene. *Black Ice.* New York: Knopf, 1991. IL: 8-9+.

Cepeda, Orlando. *My Ups and Downs in Baseball.* New York: Putnam, 1968. IL: 7-9+.

Cleary, Beverly. *The Girl from Yamhill.* New York: Morrow, 1988. IL: 5-7. RL: 7.

Collins, Michael. *Flying to the Moon and Other Strange Places.* New York: Farrar, Straus and Giroux, 1976. IL: 7-9+.

Collins, Judy. *Trust Your Heart: An Autobiography.* New York: Fawcett Crest, 1989. IL: 8-9+.

Dahl, Ronald. *Boy: Tales of Childhood.* New York: Farrar, Straus and Giroux, 1984. IL: 5-8; RL: 6.

David, Jay. *Black Roots: An Anthology.* New York: Lothrop, Lee and Shepard, 1971. IL: 7-9+.

———. *Growing Up Black.* New York: Morrow, 1968. IL: 7-9+.

———. *Growing Up Jewish.* New York: Morrow, 1969. IL: 7-9+.

Davis, Jr., Sammy. *Yes I Can: The Story of Sammy Davis, Jr.* New York: Farrar, Straus and Giroux, 1965. IL: 7-9+.

De Angeli, Marguerite Lofft. *Butter at the Old Price: An Autobiography of Margarite De Angeli.* Garden City, NY: Doubleday, 1971. IL: 4-7.

Delaney, Sarah, and A. Elizabeth Delaney with Amy Hill. *Having Our Say: The Delany Sisters First 100 Years.* New York: Kodansha International, 1993. IL: 8+.

Des Jarlait, Patrick. *Patrick Des Jarlait: The Story of an American Indian Artist.* Minneapolis, MN: Lerner, 1975. IL: 5-8.

Ditka, Mike. *Ditka: An Autobiography.* Chicago: Bonus Books, 1986. IL: 7-9+.

Dooley, Thomas A. *Doctor Tom Dooley, My Story.* New York: Farrar, Straus and Giroux, 1962. IL: 7-9+.

Dorsett, Tony. *Running Tough: The Autobiography of Tony Dorsett.* New York: Doubleday, 1989. IL: 7-9+.

Douglas, William O. *Go East, Young Man: The Early Years: The Autobiography of William O. Douglas.* New York: Random House, 1974. IL: 7-9+.

Douglas, Frederick. *My Bondage and My Freedom.* Urbana, IL: University of Illinois Press, 1987. IL: 7-9+.

Eastman, Charles Alexander. *Indian Boyhood.* New York: Dover, 1971. IL: 7-9+.

Elizabeth, Princess of Toro. *Elizabeth of Toro: The Odyssey of an African Princess: An Autobiography.* New York: Simon and Schuster, 1989. IL: 7-9+.

Fast, Howard. *Being Red: A Memoir.* Boston: Houghton Mifflin, 1990. IL: 7-9+.

Feelings, Tom. *Black Pilgrimage.* New York: Lothrop, Lee and Shepard, 1972. IL: 7-9+.

Fluek, Toby Knobel. *Memories of My Life in a Polish Village, 1930-1949.* New York: Knopf, 1990. IL: 7-9+.

Franklin, Benjamin. *The Autobiography of Benjamin Franklin.* New York: Collier, 1982. IL: 7-9+.

Fritz, Jean. *Homesick: My Own Story.* New York: Putnam, 1982. IL: 4-7; RL: 4.

Fussell, Samuel Wilson. *Muscle: Confessions of an Unlikely Bodybuilder.* New York: Poseidon, 1991. IL: 7-9+.

Gallo, Donald R. *Speaking for Ourselves, Too: More Autobiographical Sketches by Notable Authors of Books for Young Adults*. Urbana, IL: National Council for Teachers of English, 1993. IL: 7-9.

Gandhi, Mahatma. *Autobiography: The Story of My Experiments with Truth*. New York: Dover, 1983. IL: 7-9+.

Geyer, Georgie Anne. *Buying the Night Flight: The Autobiography of a Woman Foreign Correspondent*. New York: Delacorte, 1983. IL: 7-9+.

Gibson, Althea. *I Always Wanted to Be Somebody*. New York: Harper, 1958. IL: 7-9+.

Gilbreth, Frank B. *Cheaper by the Dozen*. New York: Crowell, 1963. IL: 7-9+.

Goodall, Jane. *My Life with the Chimpanzees*. New York: Pocket Books, 1988. IL: 4-7; RL: 5.

Gordy, Berry. *Movin' Up: Pop Gordy Tells His Story*. New York: Harper and Row, 1979. IL: 7-9+.

Greer, Rosey. *Rosey: An Autobiography: The Gentle Giant*. Tulsa, OK: Honor Books, 1986. IL: 6-8.

Gregory, Dick. *Nigger: An Autobiography*. New York: Washington Square Books, 1986. IL: 8-9+.

Hannam, Charles. *A Boy in That Situation: An Autobiography*. New York: Harper and Row, 1978. IL: 6-9.

Hautiz, Esther. *The Endless Steppe*. New York: Scholastic Permabound, 1981. IL: 5-8.

Hawksworth, Henry. *The Five of Me: The Autobiography of a Multiple Personality*. Chicago: Regnery, 1977. IL: 8-9+.

Hays, Helen. *My Life in Three Acts*. New York: Harcourt Brace Jovanovich, 1990. IL: 7-9+.

Henson, Matthew Alexander. *Black Explorer at the North Pole*. Lincoln, NE: University of Nebraska Press, 1989. IL: 7-9+.

Herriot, James. *All Creatures Great and Small*. New York: St. Martin's Press, 1972. IL: 7-9+.

————. *All Things Bright and Beautiful*. New York: St. Martin's Press, 1974. IL: 7-9+.

Heymanns, Betty. *Bittersweet Triumph*. Garden City, NY: Doubleday, 1977. IL: 7-9+.

Houston, Jeanne, and James D. Houston. *Farewell to Manzanar*. New York: Bantam, 1973. IL: 7-9+.

Jackson, Reggie. *Reggie: An Autobiography*. New York: Villiard Books, 1984. IL: 7-9+.

Keller, Helen. *The Story of My Life*. New York: Bantam, 1988. IL: 6-8; RL: 8.

Kherdian, David. *Root River Run*. Minneapolis, MN: Carolrhoda, 1984. IL: 5-8; RL: 6.

Kusz, Natalie. *Road Song*. New York: Farrar, Straus and Giroux, 1990. IL: 7-9+.

Landry, Tom. *Tom Landry: An Autobiography.* Grand Rapids, MI: Zondervan/ HarperCollins, 1990. IL: 7-9+.

Lim, Sing. *West Coast Chinese Boy.* Plattsburgh, NY: Tundra, 1979. IL: 4-7; RL: 7.

Little, Jean. *Little by Little: A Writer's Education.* New York: Viking Kestrel, 1987. IL: 5-8; RL: 6.

MacKinnon, Christy. *Silent Observer.* Washington, DC: Gallaudet University Press, 1993. IL: 5-8.

Malvin, John. *North Into Freedom: Autobiography of John Malvin, Free Negro, 1795-1880.* Kent, OH: Kent State University Press, 1988. IL: 7-9+.

Maiorama, Robert. *Worlds Apart: The Autobiography of a Dancer.* New York: Coward McCann and Geoghegan, 1980. IL: 8-9+.

Mays, Willie. *Say Hey: The Autobiography of Willie Mays.* New York: Simon and Schuster, 1988. IL: 7-9+.

Meltzer, Milton. *Starting from Home: A Writer's Beginnings.* New York: Viking Kestrel, 1988. IL: 7-9+; RL: 6.

Moody, Ralph. *Little Britches: Father and I Were Ranchers.* New York: Norton, 1950. IL: 4-7.

Morris, Willie. *Good Old Boy: A Delta Boyhood.* Oxford, MS: Yoknapatawpha Press, 1980. IL: 6-9.

Nakamoto, Hiroko. *My Japan, 1930-1951.* New York: McGraw, 1970. IL: 7-9+.

Naylor, Phyllis. *How I Came to Be a Writer.* New York: Macmillan, 1987. IL: 7-9+.

Nesbit, E. *Long Ago When I Was Young.* New York: Dial Books, 1988. IL: 4-7.

Neville, Emily Cheney. *Traveler from a Small Kingdom.* New York: Harper and Row, 1968. IL: 5-8.

North, Sterling. *Little Rascal.* New York: Dutton, 1965. IL: 4-7.

————. *Rascal: A Memoir of a Better Age.* New York: Dutton, 1984. IL: 5-8.

O'Kelley, Mattie Lou. *From the Hills of Georgia: An Autobiography in Paintings.* Boston: Little Brown, 1983. IL: 6-8+.

Olivier, Laurence. *Confessions of an Actor: An Autobiography.* New York: Simon and Schuster, 1982. IL: 8-9+.

Owens, Jesse. *The Jesse Owens Story.* New York: Putnam, 1970. IL: 7-9+.

Paige, Satchel. *Maybe I'll Pitch Forever: A Great Baseball Player Tells the Hilarious Story Behind the Legend.* Garden City, NY: Doubleday, 1962. IL: 7-9+.

Parcells, Bill. *Parcells: Autobiography of the Biggest Giant of Them All.* Chicago: Bonus Books, 1987. IL: 7-9+.

Paton, Alan. *Towards the Mountain: An Autobiography.* New York: Scribner, 1980. IL: 8-9+.

Peet, Bill. *Bill Peet: An Autobiography.* Boston: Houghton Mifflin, 1989. IL: 4-7; RL: 8.

Reeves, Dan. *Reeves: An Autobiography.* Chicago: Bonus Books, 1988. IL: 7-9+.

Reiss, Johanna. *The Journey Back.* New York: Crowell/HarperCollins, 1976. IL: 5-8.

————. *The Upstairs Room.* New York: Crowell/HarperCollins, 1972. IL: 4-7; RL: 5.

Richter, Hans Peter. *I Was There.* New York: Holt Rinehart and Winston, 1972. IL: 5-8.

Riis, Jacob A. *The Making of an American.* New York: Macmillan, 1970. IL: 7-9+.

Robertson, Dougal. *Survive the Savage Sea.* New York: Praeger, 1973. IL: 7-9.

Robinson, Jackie. *Breakthrough to the Big League: The Story of Jackie Robinson.* New York: Marshall Cavendish, 1991. IL: 5-8.

————. *I Never Had It Made.* New York: Putnam, 1972. IL: 7-9.

Rodgers, Pepper. *Pepper!: The Autobiography of an Unconventional Coach.* Garden City, NY: Doubleday, 1976. IL: 7-9+.

Rodriguez, Richard. *Hunger of Memory: The Education of Richard Rodriguez: An Autobiography.* New York: Bantam Books, 1983. IL: 7-9+.

Roosevelt, Eleanor. *The Autobiography of Eleanor Roosevelt.* New York: Harper, 1961. IL: 7-9+.

Ross, Pat. *Young and Female: Turning Points in the Lives of Eight American Women, Personal Accounts.* New York: Random House, 1972. IL: 7-9+.

Rylant, Cynthia. *But I'll Be Back Again: An Album.* New York: Orchard Books, 1989. IL: 7-9+; RL: 7.

Sadat, Anwar. *In Search of Identify, An Autobiography.* New York: Harper and Row, 1977. IL: 8-9+.

Sandburg, Carl. *Always the Young Strangers.* New York: Harcourt Brace, 1953. IL: 5-8.

Shears, Sarah. *A Village Girl: Memories of a Kentish Childhood.* New York: Simon and Schuster, 1972. IL: 6-8.

Singer, Isaac Bashevis. *A Day of Pleasure: Stories of a Boy Growing Up in Warsaw.* New York: Farrar, Straus and Giroux, 1969. IL: 6-9+.

Sleator, William. *Oddballs.* New York: Dutton Child Books, 1993. IL: 7-9.

Someth, May. *Cambodian Witness: An Autobiography of Someth May.* New York: Random House, 1987. IL: 7-9+.

Stargill, Willie. *Willie Stargill: An Autobiography.* New York: Harper, 1984. IL: 6-8+.

Steffens, Joseph Lincoln. *Boy on Horseback.* New York: Harcourt, 1963. IL: 6-8+.

Stevenson, James. *When I Was Nine.* New York: Greenwillow, 1986. IL: 3-5; RL: 4.

Sullivan, Tom. *If You Could See What I Hear.* New York: Harper and Row, 1975. IL: 7-9+.

Takashima, Shizuye. *A Child in Prison Camp.* Chicago: Childrens Press, 1971. IL: 5-8; RL: 5.

Thurber, James. *My Life and Hard Times.* New York: Harper and Row, 1973. IL: 7-9+.

Twain, Mark. *The Autobiography of Mark Twain Including Chapters Now Published for the First Time.* New York: Harper, 1959. IL: 7-9+.

Unitas, Johnny. *Pro Quarterback: My Own Story*. New York: Simon and Schuster, 1965. IL: 7-9+.

Washington, Booker Taliafero. *Up from Slavery: An Autobiography*. New York: Dodd, Mead, 1965. IL: 7-9+.

Watkins, Yoko Kawashima. *So Far from the Bamboo Garden*. New York: Lothrop, Lee and Shepard, 1986. IL: 7-9+.

Wayne, Kyra Petrovska. *Shurik, A Story of the Seige of Leningrad*. New York: Grosset, 1970. IL: 6-9.

White, Ryan. *Ryan White: My Own Story*. New York: Dial Books for Young Readers, 1991. IL: 5-8; RL: 5.

Whyte, Edna Gardner. *Rising Above It: The Autobiography of Edna Gardner Whyte*. New York: Crown/Orion, 1991. IL: 8-9+.

Williams, Ted. *My Turn at Bat: The Story of My Life*. New York: Simon and Schuster, 1969. IL: 5-8+.

Wojciechowska, Maia. *Till the Break of Day*. New York: Harcourt Brace Jovanovich, 1972. IL: 5-8.

Wong, Jade Snow. *Fifth Chinese Daughter*. Seattle, WA: University of Washington Press, 1989. IL: 4-7.

Worden, Alfred Merrill. *I Want To Know About a Flight to the Moon*. Garden City, NY: Doubleday, 1974. IL: 5-7.

Written by Herself: Autobiographies of American Women: An Anthology. New York: Vintage Books, 1992. IL: 8-9+.

X, Malcolm. *The Autobiography of Malcolm X*. New York: Ballantine Books, 1973. IL: 7-9+.

Yeager, Chuck. *Yeager, An Autobiography*. New York: Bantam Books, 1985. IL: 7-9+.

Yep, Laurence. *Lost Garden*. New York: Messner, 1991. IL: 5-8; RL: 7.

Zemach, Margot. *Self-Portrait: Margot Zemach*. New York: Harper, 1978. IL: 4-7; RL: 6.

Zlata, Filipovic. *Zlata's Diary: A Child's Life in Sarajevo*. New York: Viking, 1994. IL: 5-8.

Professional Sources

Collecting information about personal or cultural events that use interview techniques can be used in many ways to elicit student interest and to motivate children to read and write. There are many sources of information about oral history. Those listed here are more specific to this particular activity. For a complete look at the topic, search for information under terms such as *oral history, family history,* and *interview techniques.*

Ahren, John. "Teaching Oral History Techniques." *OCSS Review* 26, no. 1 (Spring 1990), pp. 39-44.

Balkwell, Carolyn, and Roberta L. Null. "Oral History as an Integrative Teaching Strategy for Home Economics." *Illinois Teacher of Home Economics* 29, no. 5 (May-June 1986), pp.174-75.

Blount, H. Parker. "Making History Live for Secondary Students: Infusing People into the Narrative." *Social Studies* 83, no. 5 (September-October 1992), pp. 220-223.

Cheek, Jr., Earl H. "Family Folklore Sparks Reading." *Reading Teacher* 42, no. 9 (May 1989), p. 737.

Clegg, Luther B., et al. "Creating Oral History Projects for the Social Studies Classroom." *Social Studies Review* 32, no. 1 (Fall 1992), pp. 53-60.

Daly, Richard F. *Oral History: Its Background, Definition, and Interview Types.* Minnesota, 1984. ED 237380.

Foxfire: 25 Years. New York: Doubleday, 1991.

Havlice, Patricia Pate. *Oral History: A Reference Guide and Annotated Bibliography.* Jefferson, NC: McFarland, 1985.

Hawkins, Carria. *Teaching Reading Through Oral Histories.* Philadelphia, PA: Lutheran Mission Society/Pennsylvania State Department of Education, 1984. ED 260277.

Hirshfield, Claire. "New Worlds from Old: An Experience in Oral History at the Elementary School Level." *Social Studies* 82, no. 3 (May-June 1991), pp. 110-14.

Kachaturoff, Grace, and Frances Greenebaum. "Oral History in the Social Studies Classroom." *Social Studies* 72, no. 1 (January-February 1981), pp. 18-22.

Kazemek, Francis E. "Stories of Our Lives: Interviews and Oral Histories for Language Development." *Journal of Reading* 29, no. 3 (December 1985), pp. 211-18.

King, James R., and Norman A. Stahl. *Oral History as a Critical Pedagogy: Some Cautionary Issues.* Paper presented at the annual meeting of the American Reading Forum, Sarasota, FL, December 12-15, 1990. ED 333492.

Kotkin, Amy J., and Holly C. Baker. "Family Folklore." *Childhood Education* (January 1977), pp. 137-42.

Lanman, Barry A. "Oral History as an Educational Tool for Teaching Immigration and Black History in American High Schools: Findings and Queries. *International Journal of Oral History* 8, no. 2 (June 1987), pp. 122-35.

Lanman, Barry Allen, and George L. Mehaffy. *Oral History in the Secondary School Classroom.* Provo, UT: Oral History Association, 1988.

Lehane, Stephen, and Richard Goldman. "Oral History: Research and Teaching Tool for Educators." *Elementary School Journal* 77, no. 3 (January 1977), pp. 173-81.

Mehaffy, George L., et al. *Oral History in the Classroom: How To Do It Series, Series 2, No. 8.* Washington, DC: National Council for the Social Studies, 1979.

Nelson, Murry, and H. Wells Singleton. "Using Oral History in the Social Studies Classroom." *Social Studies Journal* 5, no. 1 (Winter 1975-1976), pp. 42-50.

Neuenschwander, John A. *Oral History as a Teaching Approach.* Washington, DC: National Education Association, 1976.

Oral History in the Secondary School Classroom. Los Angeles, CA: Oral History Association, 1988. ED 348330.

Oral History: What? Why? How? Guidelines for Oral History. Harrisburg, PA: Pennsylvania State Dept. of Education, 1975. ED 117014.

Ryant, Carl. "Oral History and the Family: A Tool for the Documentation and Interpretation of Family History." *Teaching History: A Journal of Methods* 15, no. 2 (Fall 1990), pp. 51-56.

Schipper, Stuart P. *Oral History: An Effective Means To Enhance Education in the Elementary Classroom.* Indiana, 1982. ED 224744.

Sitton, Thad. "Oral Life History: From Tape Recorder to Typewriter." *Social Studies* 72, no. 3 (May-June 1981), pp. 120-26.

Stahl, Mark B. "Using Traditional Oral Stories in the English Classroom." *English Journal* 68, no. 7 (October 1979), pp. 33-36.

Sullivan, Margaret L., and Irene E. Cortinovis. "Oral History Recorded and Recycled." *Teaching History* 2, no. 1 (Spring 1977), pp. 28-31.

Thavenet, Dennis J. *Family History: Coming Face-to-Face with the Past. How To Do It, Series 2, No. 15.* Washington, DC: National Council for the Social Studies, 1981.

Wieder, Alan. "Oral History in the Classroom: An Exploratory Essay." *Social Studies* 75, no. 2 (March-April 1984), pp. 71-74.

Wigginton, Eliot. *Sometimes a Shining Moment: The Foxfire Experience.* Garden City, NY: Anchor Press/Doubleday, 1985.

FABLES AND PROVERBS

Fables are narratives or stories with a moral emphasis. Most published American and English fables state the moral at the end of the story. The fabulist is a storyteller whose aim is to study human nature in general. Human nature is shown at its "lowest common denominator" through brief stories, often with personified animals who portray certain conduct or character. Plots are reduced to the barest of sequential details. The language, especially adjectives that describe the characters, contributes to a general stereotype of a particular kind of conduct or aspect of human nature. There is usually little description that is not related to the teaching or study. The fable shares some characteristics with the allegory, a story that uses symbols to portray a particular religious or political doctrine; the parable, a short narrative presented as an analogy; the proverb, a short, well-known statement expressing a truth, fact, concept, or ideal; and the exemplum, a story claiming to be an accurate example illustrating a point.

In Western tradition, the fable begins in the sixth century B.C. with Aesop, whose stories have been told and retold for centuries. Aesop's life story has come to take on legendary proportions with several variations. In the fifth century, Herodutus wrote that Aesop was a Greek slave who lived in the sixth century. In the first century A.D., Plutarch recorded that Aesop was an adviser to Croesus, King of Lydia. Another version states that Aesop was from Thrace, and yet another, that he was from the island of Samos. Whoever Aesop was, a real person or combination of individuals, the stories have provided a basis for the written fable in the West.

In the first century A.D., Phaedrus produced a fable-like story in Rome that greatly influenced writers including La Fontaine in the 17th century.

Other fabulists, such as the Roman poet Horace, the Greek biographer Plutarch, and the Greek satirist Lucian, produced also these brief stories. Fable writing continued in Middle Ages as exemplified by a collection from Marie de France in the twelfth century. These fables and other allegorical stories evolved into the beast epic, a long story of heroes and villains, such as Reynard the Fox.

The fable as a literary form peaked in France with La Fontaine during the seventeenth century. His first collection, *Fables*, was published in 1668 and followed the Aesop pattern, especially from the time of Phaedrus. The second collection was longer and drew from other sources such as the Indian Pilpay. La Fontaine's later fables satirized the French court, church, and nobility.

Other fabulists followed. In the Romantic period came the Russian Ivan Andreyevich Krylov. The eastern tradition began in India with the fifth century collection of beast fables first recorded in the *Pancatantra,* and surviving in a Sanskrit version, *Kalilah wa Dimnah.* Buddhists adapted these stories in China and Japan.

For the teacher, library media specialist, or parent, fables, whether in prose or verse form, can be used to introduce students to other literary forms, such as story poetry, which is a story embellished as a folktale and excerpted from legends or myths. The retelling of fables is easy because of their brevity. As mentioned earlier, the main language characteristics include the personification of animals, whose actions emerge from the simple incident or series of incidents. The particular moral study or lesson generally takes the form of a proverb. It will be of interest to students that many cultures have fables that are similar, but which provide slightly different lessons. Sometimes it seems that fables provide contradictory lessons. This may intrigue students who are beginning to question life and who will be interested in the way in which certain events are interpreted. Because a fable espouses a particular moral or code of conduct, students have an opportunity to become involved in thinking about how difficult it is to find beliefs shared by all of humanity. A study of fables allows students to think about their own moral beliefs and standards, whether they agree with the moral lesson of a fable, and to write about it or even to create their own fables.

Professional Sources

The books and articles in the list that follows contain suggested fables and information about fables and how to use them with children and young adults.

Aesop: Five Centuries of Illustrated Fables. New York: Metropolitan Museum of Art, 1964.

Allen, Virginia French. *Aesop and Company: Using Traditional Tales in EFL Classes.* Paper presented at the conference of International Association of Teachers of English as a Foreign Language, Oxford, England, January 1977. ED 139298.

Arora, Shirley L. "A Critical Bibliography of Mexican American Proverbs." *Aztlan-International Journal of Chicano Studies Research* 13, nos. 1-2 (Spring-Fall 1982), pp. 71-80.

———. "Proverbs in Mexican American Tradition." *Aztlan-International Journal of Chicano Studies Research* 13, nos. 1-2 (Spring-Fall 1982), pp. 43-69.

Barnet, Judith M. "Folk Wit and Wisdom." *Intercom* 90-91 (December 1978), pp. 14-18.

Bennett, Charles H. *Bennett's Fables from Aesop and Others: Translated into Human Nature.* New York: Viking, 1978.

Baird, Jeane D. *The Style of La Fontaine's Fables.* Scranton, PA: Barnes and Noble, 1966.

Blackham, H. J. *The Fable as Literature.* London: Athlone, 1985.

Caldecott, Randolph. *The Caldecott Aesop: A Facsimile of the 1883 Edition.* New York: Macmillan, 1978.

Chance, Jane. *The Mythographic Art: Classical Fable and the Rise of the Vernacular in Early France and England.* Gainesville, FL: University of Florida Press, 1990.

Daniel, Jack L., et al. "Makin' a Way Outa No Way: The Proverb Tradition in the Black Experience." *Journal of Black Studies* 17, no. 4 (June 1987), pp. 482-508.

DeMourgues, Odette. *Fables by La Fontaine: Critical Analysis.* Woodbury, NY: Barron's Educational Series, 1960.

Fables: Literature Curriculum, Levels C-D. Grades Three and Four. Teacher's Guide. Eugene, OR: University of Oregon Press, 1971. ED 075842.

Feichtl, Nancy Gibbons Cullen. *Using Proverbs to Facilitate Metaphorical Language Comprehension: A Curriculum Study.* Doctoral dissertation, University of Maryland, College Park, 1988.

Folk, Judith. *Around the World through Stories: An Annotated Bibliography of Folk Literature.* Honolulu, HI: Hawaii University Press, 1990. ED 309779.

Goetz-Stankiewicz, Marketa. "The Fable and Power Play: Thoughts on a Recurring Theme," in *Literary History, Narrative, and Culture*, eds. Wimal Dissanayake and Steven Bradbury. Honolulu, HI: University of Hawaii Press, 1989.

————. "The Sheep in Wolf's Clothing: Thoughts on Modern Variations of an Ancient Fable," in *From Sign to Text: A Semiotic View of Communication*, ed. Yishai Tobin. Amsterdam: Benjamins, 1989.

Goldman, Susan. *Use of Prior Knowledge in Understanding Fables in First and Second Languages.* Paper presented at the annual meeting of American Educational Research Association, Montreal, Quebec, April 11-14, 1983. ED 233571

Goodwin, Paul D., and Joseph W. Henzel. "Proverbs and Practical Reasoning: A Study in Socio-Logic." *Quarterly Journal of Speech* 65, no. 3 (October 1979), pp. 289-302.

Gottlieb, Robin. "Jean de la Fontaine and Children." *Horn Book*, no. 1 (February 1983), pp. 25-32.

Guiton, Margaret. *La Fontaine: Poet and Counter-Poet.* New Brunswick, NJ: Rutgers University Press, 1961.

Guthrie, John. "Research Views: Fables." *Reading Teacher* 31. no. 6 (March 1978), pp. 724-26.

Hedges, Ned Samuel. *The Fable and the Fabulous: The Use of Traditional Forms in Children's Literature.* Doctoral dissertation, University of Nebraska, 1968. University Microfilms No. 68-18020.

Henderson, Arnold Clayton. "Animal Fables as Vehicles of Social Protest and Satire: Twelfth Century to Henryson," in *Third International Beast Epic, Fable and Fabliau Colloquium, Munster 1979, Proceedings*, eds. Jan Goossens and Timothy Sodman. Cologne: Bohlau, 1981.

————. "Medieval Beasts and Modern Cages: The Making of Meaning in Fables and Beastiaries." *PMLA: Publications of the Modern Language Association* 97, no. 1 (January 1982), pp. 40-49.

Herman, Gertrude. "A Picture Is Worth a Thousand Words." *Horn Book Magazine* 62, no. 6 (November-December 1986), pp. 758-59.

Hood, Susan. "Arnold Lobel's Fables." *Instructor* 90, no. 10 (May 1981), pp. 34-39.

Jose, Paul E. *Development of the Appreciation of Fables.* Paper presented at the biennial meeting of the Society for Research in Child Development, Baltimore, MD, April 23-26, 1987. ED 283610.

Kei-ichiro, Kobori. "Aesop in the East and West." *Tamkang Review: A Quarterly of Comparative Studies Between Chinese and Foreign Literatures* 14, nos. 1-4 (Autumn-Summer 1983-1984), pp. 101-13.

Kitzhaber, Albert. *Fables, Parables, Short Stories—Literature Curriculum 1, Teacher Version*. Eugene, OR: University of Oregon Press, 1965. ED 010138.

Knoespel, Kenneth J. "Fable and the Epistemology of Expanding Narrative: An Example from the Roman de la Rose." *University of Hartford Studies in Literature: A Journal of Interdisciplinary Criticism* 17, no. 2 (1985), pp. 28-48.

Kordecki, Lesley. "Fables: The Moral of the Study," in *Teaching the Middle Ages II*, eds. Robert Graybill, John Hallwas, Judy Hample, Robert Kindrick, and Robert Lovell. Warrensburg, MO: Central Missouri State University Press, 1985.

Lutzer, Victoria B. "Comprehension of Proverbs by Average Children and Children with Learning Disorders." *Journal of Learning Disabilities* 21, no. 2 (February 1988), pp. 104-108.

Manzo, Anthony V. "Using Proverbs To Teach Reading and Thinking; or Come Forceva Mia Monno (The Way My Grandmother Did It)." *Reading Teacher* 34. no. 4 (January 1981), pp. 411-16.

Martin, Louis. "The 'Aesop' Fable-Animal," in *On Signs*, ed. Marshall Blonsky. Baltimore, MD: Johns Hopkins University Press, 1985.

McKenna, John F. "The Proverb in Humanistic Studies: Language, Literature and Culture: Theory and Classroom Practice." *French Review* 48, no. 2 (December 1974), pp. 377-91.

Meixner, Linda L. "Proverbs: Worldly Wisdom." *Religion and Public Education* 17, no. 1 (Winter 1990), pp. 119-25.

Mieder, Wolfgang. *Tradition and Innovation in Folk Literature*. Hanover, NH: University Press of New England, 1987.

Mirel, Barbara. "Tradition and the Individual Retelling." *Children's Literature Association Quarterly* 9, no. 2 (Summer 1984), pp. 63-66.

Moss, Judy. "The Fable and Critical Thinking." *Language Arts* 57, no. 1 (January 1980), pp. 21-29.

Needler, Howard. "The Animal Fable Among Other Medieval Literary Genres." *New Literary History: A Journal of Theory and Interpretation* 22, no. 2 (Spring 1991), pp. 423-39.

Pflieger, Pat. "Fables into Picture Books." *Children's Literature Association Quarterly* 9, no. 2 (Summer 1984), pp. 73-75, 80.

Pillar, Arlene M. "Aspects of Moral Judgement in Response to Fables." *Journal of Research and Development in Education* 16. no. 3 (Spring 1983), pp. 39-46.

———. *Dimensions of the Development of Moral Judgement as Reflected in Children's Responses to Fables*. Research paper prepared at New York University, 1980. ED 205889.

————. *Look Before You Leap: Fables for the Elementary Level.* Paper presented at the annual meeting of the National Council of Teachers of English, Cincinnati, OH, November 16-21, 1980. ED 196028.

Provenzo, Eugene Francis. *Education and the Aesopic Tradition.* ED 131462.

Reinstein, P. Gila. "Aesop and Grimm: Contrast in Ethical Codes and Contemporary Values." *Children's Literature in Education* 14, no. 1 (Spring 1983), pp. 44-53.

Rosenfeld, Judith. "Retelling Fabulous Fables." *Yarnspinner* 16, no. 1 (February 1992), pp. 1-2.

Sauvageau, Juan. *Fabulas para Siempre. Volume One.* Boise, ID: Twin Pines Editorial, 1979. ED 201440.

Scorza, Richard. "Text and Interpretation: A Teaching Strategy." *Teaching English in a Two-Year College* 6, no. 2 (Winter 1980), pp. 105-106.

Shannon, Patrick, et al. "An Investigation of Children's Ability to Comprehend Character Motives." *American Educational Research Journal* 25, no. 3 (Fall 1988), pp. 441-62.

Shapiro, Norman R., and David Schorr. *The Fabulists French: Verse Fables of Nine Centuries.* Urbana, IL: University of Illinois Press, 1992.

Skibell, Cindy. "Dramatizing Fables and Skits." *Foreign Language Annals* 9, no. 3 (May 1976), pp. 240-41.

Taylor, Mary-Agnes. "The Literary Transformation of a Sluggard." *Children's Literature: An International Journal, Inc., Annual of the Modern Language Association Division on Children's Literature* 12 (1984), pp. 92-104.

Thistle, Louise. *Dramatizing Aesop's Fables: Creative Scripts for the Elementary Classroom.* Palo Alto, CA: Dale Seymour Publications, 1993.

Turner, Nigel E., and Albert N. Katz. *Context Effects in Comprehending Familiar and Unfamiliar Proverbs.* Paper presented at annual meeting of the Psychometric Society, New Orleans, LA, November 14-18, 1990.

U. S. Library of Congress. *General Reference and Bibliography Division. Fables from Incunabula to Modern Picture Books—A Selective Bibliography.* Washington, DC: Library of Congress, 1966.

Wadsworth, Philip A. "The Art of Allegory in La Fontaine's Fables." *French Review* 45, no. 6 (May 1972), pp. 1125-35.

Wolkomir, Richard. "A Proverb a Day Keeps This Scholar at Play." *Smithsonian* 23, no. 6 (September 1992), pp.111-18.

Ziolkowski, Jan M. "The Form and Spirit of the Beast Fable." *Beastia: Yearbook of the Beast Fable Society* 2 (May 1990), pp. 4-18.

Associations

Beast Fable Society, North East Missouri State University, Kirksville, MO 63501, Ben Bennani, ed.

Activity: Writing from Proverb to Fable

The intent of the fabulist is that a lesson be learned. If the story is sufficiently understandable, the students' prior knowledge will help in the transfer of new learning or insight. What happens when the student is required to be the author? The moral or lesson is provided first and the story is created to support that moral.

To begin this activity, read some fables to the students or have them read them on their own. As they listen or read, direct them to think about the moral teaching or lesson usually found at the end of the fable. Introduce students to reference books that contain proverbs. Invite them to discuss the particular sayings that they find meaningful or that have proven true in their own lives.

Suggest that this exercise provides an opportunity for students to become the storyteller or to adopt the role of "Aesop." Select and display several proverbs or sayings, some that you are sure students will be familiar with and others that are likely to be new. Build your own list on the suggestions that follow.

- Don't count your chicks before they're hatched.
- Don't put all your eggs into one basket.
- Different strokes for different folks.
- One picture is worth a thousand words.
- A woman's place is in the home.
- Out of sight, out of mind.
- Early to bed, early to rise makes a man healthy, wealthy, and wise.

Encourage students to add proverbs they know to the list. Invite each student to select one of the proverbs and visualize it. What image does the proverb bring to mind. How does the image provide meaning? Does the image suggest a story?

As students think about the proverbs, offer some examples to help them with the process. Share a fable from one of the books in the resources list. There are excellent versions of Aesop's fables and some less traditional stories as well. Have students identify the lesson or proverb contained in the fable first. Then help them look at the details of the story.

Allow students time to consider the mental picture that has surfaced from reflecting on one of the proverbs or sayings. What might happen that would lead to the lesson implied in the proverb? Have students write out in a logical sequence a list of possibilities. From this list, instruct them to write out a story, filling in the details needed to make the story interesting.

The completed drafts may be read aloud and edited for spelling, grammar, and logic. The fables may be typed and illustrated with photographs from magazines or line drawings of their own creation.

Student Sources: Fables

Fables can be found in picture books and easy-to-read versions, illustrated by artists such as Lorinda Bryan Cauley, Paul Galdone, Janet Stevens, and Ed Young, to name a few. Although such picture book formats may be appropriate for the adolescent reader, they have not been included in this list. The titles selected in the following list require a higher reading ability, however, than picture books. In these books, the stories strongly infer a moral lesson. Some of these books are currently out of print but can still be found in library collections. Check catalogs and folklore indexes for other recommendations. IL represents the interest level and RL represents the Fry readability level of the book, where available.

Print

Aesop's Fables. Illustrated by Michael Hague. New York: Henry Holt, 1985. IL: 3-6; RL: 6.

Aesop's Fables. Illustrated by Heidi Holder. New York: Viking, 1981. IL: 4-8.

Aesop's Fables. Illustrated by Arthur Rackham. New York: Watts, 1968. IL: 5-8.

Aesop's Fables. Illustrated by Charles Santore. New York: Jellybean/Crowell, 1988. IL: 4-7; RL: 6.

Anderson, Rachel, and David Bradby. *Reynard the Fox.* New York: Oxford, 1986. IL: 5-8; RL: 6.

Anno, Mitsumasa. *Anno's Aesop: A Book of Fables by Aesop and Mr. Fox.* New York: Orchard/Watts, 1989. IL: 3-6; RL: 5.

Arnott, Kathleen. *Animal Folktales Around the World.* New York: Walck, 1970. IL: 4-7.

Ash, Russell, and Bernard Highton. *Aesop's Fables.* San Francisco, CA: Chronicle Books, 1990. IL: 4-8.

Babbitt, Ellen C. *Jakata Tales.* New York: Appleton Century Crofts, 1940. IL: 5-8.

———. *More Jakata Tales.* New York: Appleton Century Crofts, 1955. IL: 5-8.

Bader, Barbara. *Aesop and Company: With Scenes from His Legendary Life.* Illustrated by Arthur Geisert. Boston: Houghton Mifflin, 1991. IL: 5-8.

Belloc, Hilaire. *Matilda Who Told Lies and Was Burned to Death.* New York: Knopf, 1992. IL: 7-9.

Bennett, Charles. *Bennett's Fables from Aesop and Others, Translated into Human Nature.* New York: Viking, 1978. IL: 5-9.

Bennett, William. *The Book of Virtues: A Treasury of Great Moral Stories*. New York: Simon and Schuster, 1993. IL: 7-9.

Bierhorst, John. *Doctor Coyote: A Native American's Aesop's Fables*. New York: Macmillan, 1987. IL: 3-6; RL: 3.

Caldecott Aesop. Garden City, NY: Doubleday, 1978. IL: 6-8+.

Calder, Alexander. *Fables of Aesop According to Sir Roger L'Estrange*. New York: Dover, 1967. IL: 3-6.

Carrick, Valery. *Still More Russian Picture Tales*. New York: Dover, 1970. IL: 4-6.

Cooney, Barbara. *Chanticleer and the Fox*. New York: Crowell/HarperCollins, 1958. IL: 2-6; RL: 6.

Demi. *Chinese Zoo: Fables and Proverbs*. New York: Harcourt Brace Jovanovich, 1987. IL: 3-6; RL: 6.

———. *Demi's Reflective Fables*. New York: Grosset & Dunlap, 1988. IL: 5-8; RL: 6.

DeRoin Nancy. *Jataka Tales*. Boston: Houghton Mifflin, 1975. IL: 3-7.

Durr, Gisela. *Aesop's Fables*. New York: North-South Books, 1995. IL: 3-6.

Gaer, Joseph. *Fables of India*. Boston: Little, Brown, 1955. IL: 4-7.

Hastings, Selina. *Reynard the Fox*. Illustrated by Graham Percy. New York: Tamborine Books, 1991. IL: 4-7.

Heide, Florence Parry, and Sylvia Worth Van Clief. *Fables You Shouldn't Pay Any Attention To*. Philadelphia: Lippincott, 1978. IL: 4-7.

Jacobs, Joseph. *The Fables of Aesop, Told Anew, and Their History Traced by Joseph Jacobs*. New York: Schocken, 1964. IL: 4-7; RL: 4.

Kamen, Gloria. *The Ringdoves: From the Fables of Bidpai*. New York: Atheneum, 1988. IL: 5-8.

Krylov, Ivan Andreevich. *15 Fables of Krylov*. New York: Macmillan, 1965. IL: 4-7.

La Fontaine, Jean. *Selected Fables*. New York: Dover, 1968. IL: 5-8.

Lewis, Naomi. *Cry Wolf and Other Aesop Fables*. Illustrated by Barry Castle. New York: Oxford University Press, 1988. IL: 5-8.

Lionni, Leo. *Frederick's Fables*. New York: Random House, 1985. IL: 3-7.

Lobel, Arnold. *Fables*. New York: Harper and Row, 1980. IL: 3-6; RL: 5.

Mathias, Robert. *Aesop's Fables*. Morristown, NJ: Silver Burdette, 1986. IL: 4-8.

McClintock, Barbara. *Animal Fables from Aesop*. Boston: David R. Godine, 1991. IL: 4-7.

McKendry, John L. *Aesop: Five Centuries of Illustrated Fables*. New York: Metropolitan Museum of Art, 1964. IL: 6-8.

Nardini, Bruno. *Fables of Leonardo Da Vinci*. Northbrook, IL: Hubbard Press, 1973. IL: 6-8.

Paxton, Tom. *Aesop's Fables Retold in Verse*. New York: Morrow, 1988. IL: 4-7.

———. *Belling the Cat and Other Aesop's Fables*. New York: Morrow, 1990. IL: 4-7.

Reeves, James. *Fables from Aesop*. New York: Bedrick/Blackie, 1985. IL: 4-7; RL: 6.

Shapiro, Norman R. *Fifty Fables of La Fontaine.* Urbana, IL: University of Illinois Press, 1988. IL: 5-8.

Shaw, George Bernard. *Androcles and the Lion.* New York: Penguin, 1963. IL: 7-8.

Soyer, Abraham. *The Adventures of Yewina and Other Stories.* New York: Viking, 1979. IL: 4-7.

Storr, Catherine. *Androcles and the Lion.* Milwaukee, WI: Raintree, 1986. IL: 4-7; RL: 6.

Tinkelman, Murray. *Aesop's Fables.* New York: Doubleday, 1986. IL: 4-8.

Nonprint

Aesop Anthology. Chicago: American School Publishers, 1977. 6 sound filmstrips.

Aesop's Fables. New York: Caedmon CDL5 1221, 1967. 43 min. 1 audiocassette.

Aesop's Fables. Toronto, Ontario: Discus Knowledge Research, 1991. 1 interactive CD-ROM Disk.

Aesop's Fables. Del Mar, CA: McGraw Hill Films, 1967. 14 min. One 16mm film.

Aesop's Fables. Ho-Ho-Kus, NJ: National Cinema Service. 27 min. One 16mm film.

Aesop's Fables I. Del Mar, CA: McGraw Hill Films/ Lumin Productions, 1967. 13 min. One 16mm film.

Aesop's Fables II. Del Mar, CA: McGraw Hill Films/Lumin Productions, 1967. 11 min. One 16mm film.

Aesop's Fables III. Del Mar, CA: McGraw Hill Films/Lumin Productions, 1967. 14 min. One 16mm film.

Clever Village. Del Mar, CA: McGraw Hill Films, 1973. 10 min. One 16mm film.

Fables of Aesop. Read by John Franklin. New Rochelle, NY: Spoken Arts SA 1013, 1969. 1 sound disk.

The Hoarder. Briarcliff Manor, NY: Benchmark Films, 1972. 8 min. 1 videocassette.

Lobel, Arnold. *Fables.* Chicago: American School Publishers, 1981. 1 sound filmstrip.

Thurber, James. *The 13 Clocks.* Read by Peter Ustinov. New York: Caedmon A 2089, 1980. 79 min. 2 audiocassettes.

Student Sources: Proverbs

There are a number of books of quotations. These particular volumes include specific examples of proverbs.

Bartlett, John. *Familiar Quotations: A Collection of Passages, Phrases and Proverbs Traced to Their Sources in Ancient and Modern Literature.* Boston: Little, Brown, 1980.

Davidoff, Henry. *World Treasury of Proverbs from Twenty-Five Languages*. New York: Random House, 1946.

Fergusson, Rosalind. *Facts on File Dictionary of Proverbs*. New York: Facts on File, 1983.

Hurwitz, Johanna. *A Word to the Wise and Other Proverbs*. New York: Morrow, 1994. IL: 3-6.

King, Anita. *Quotations in Black*. Westport, CT: Greenwood Press, 1981.

Rogers, James. *A Dictionary of Cliché*. New York: Facts on File, 1985.

Simpson, J. A. *Concise Oxford Dictionary of Proverbs*. New York: Oxford University Press, 1982.

Stevenson, Burton Egbert. *The Macmillan Book of Proverbs, Maxims, and Familiar Phrases*. New York: Macmillan, 1965.

Whiting, Bartlett Jere. *Modern Proverbs and Proverbial Sayings*. Cambridge, MA: Harvard University Press, 1989.

Professional Sources

Activities in which students produce their own proverbs and fables is one way to approach the study of language. Current reading and writing practices combine the use of reading forms and modeling patterns read in the writing. The following sources are useful if the reader wishes to pursue this topic in more depth.

Brickman, Bette. "Publishing ESL Student Writing." *Teaching English in the Two-Year College* 20, no. 1 (February 1993), pp. 47-48.

D'Angelo, Frank J. "Some Uses of Proverbs." *College Composition and Communication* 28, no. 4 (1978), pp. 365-369.

Eissing, Caryl. "Proverbs in the Classroom." *Reading Teacher* 43, no. 2 (November 1989), pp. 188-89.

Holden, Marjorie H., and Mimi Warshaw. "A Bird in the Hand and a Bird in the Bush: Using Proverbs to Teach Skills and Comprehension." *English Journal* 74, no. 2 (February 1985), pp. 63-67.

Mieder, Wolfgang. *American Proverbs: A Study of Texts and Contexts*. New York: Peter Lang, 1989.

Saltz, Rosalyn. "Children's Interpretation of Proverbs." *Language Arts* 56, no. 5 (May 1979), pp. 508-14.

MYTHS

Myths are "traditional stories representing supernatural beings, ancestors, and heroes that serve as primordial types in a primitive view of the world."

Often it is difficult to distinguish between legends, myths, and folktales. Many times what is religious or what has been ascribed to a god in one version of a story is secularized in another version. What one culture takes for a simple story may have religious significance to another culture. Human heroes of legend take on godlike characteristics in some stories. How-and-why stories speak of origins but are not considered religious. One culture may tell a story about its god from a humorous point of view, using it to entertain as well as to explain about the culture's origins. Schools often teach only Greek mythology because they consider these stories to be "safe." These "safe" examples may often appear to students as nothing more than stories unrelated to the purpose of the form as a conveyer of the religious values of a group. These myths may be important in helping the students' understanding of the power that myth can have in their lives.

Characters from myths are alluded to in many narrative forms. Often it is not possible to understand certain passages in fiction without knowing the mythological stories. Writers like Jane Yolen, Alan Garner, Andre Norton, Ursula K. LeGuin, Susan Cooper, Jean Craighead George, Mary Renault, and Rosemary Sutcliff are only a few contemporary writers who allude regularly to mythological characters and events.

For the teacher, library media specialist, or parent there are many advantages to knowing mythology and being able to teach it. Today our stories are written in prose, and they arise from a variety of cultures and religious origins. Modern fantasy and science fiction owe much to ancient myth and oral tradition. Students' reading experiences are enriched when they understand that story tradition. The old stories deal with the subject of creation or beginnings as well as natural phenomena. Those stories usually represent the values of the culture from which they originate. The gods and heroes and their distinguishing traits, characteristics, and values are reported according to the importance the culture may place on them. The language used in myths requires knowledge of other stories or figures in that particular mythology. Often mythical allusions are used for comparison. The nature of the relationships and the subject matter require complex sentences. Students must be syntactically agile in reading and comprehending embedded sentence structures. Good readers and curious young people will find the exploration of myths quite satisfying. For poorer, but still curious readers, the teacher or library media specialist will need to find versions of stories that allow for the conveying of plot and character without the complexity.

Professional Sources

A number of professional sources can be used to gather materials and ideas about myth. The nature of myth has been studied in sociology, religion, and psychology, as well as literature. Materials to support an individual study are available in abundance. Several examples of types of sources that are offered for the teacher or library media specialist trying to develop a curriculum for the study of myth are included in the following list.

The first type of material includes general references, some of which provide a comprehensive overview and answer questions, such as: What role does the myth play in past and present culture? How are our myths symbols of a basic human condition? How is religion myth?

The second list of resources includes bibliographies and indexes, helpful in locating materials appropriate for use with students. These bibliographies identify print and nonprint materials that have been successfully used or are highly recommended for their literary quality or usefulness with specific audiences.

General

Campbell, Joseph. *The Masks of God: Creative Mythology*. New York: Viking, 1968.

———. *The Masks of God: Occidental Mythology*. New York: Viking.

———. *The Masks of God: Oriental Mythology*. New York: Viking, 1962.

———. *The Masks of God: Primitive Mythology*. New York: Viking, 1959.

———. *The Power of Myth*. New York: Doubleday, 1988.

Carr, Marion. "Classic Hero in a New Mythology." *The Horn Book Magazine* 47, no. 5 (October 1971), pp. 508-13.

Cliff, Janet M. "Navajo Games." *Indian Culture and Research Journal* 14, no. 3 (1990), pp. 1-81.

Clover, Carol J., and John Lindow. *Norse-Icelandic Literature: A Critical Guide*. Ithaca, NY: Cornell University Press, 1985.

Cook, Elizabeth. *The Ordinary and the Fabulous: An Introduction to Myths, Legends and Fairy Tales*. New York: Cambridge University Press, 1976.

Eliot, Alexander. *Myths*. New York: McGraw-Hill, 1976.

Moyers, Bill. *Joseph Campbell and the Power of Myth*. 1-6. London: PBS/Mystic Fire Video, 1988. Six 60-min. videotapes.

South, Malcolm. *Mythical and Fabulous Creatures: A Source Book and Research Guide*. New York: Bedrick, 1988.

Bibliographies

Boswell, Jeanetta. *"Past Ruined Illion . . .": A Bibliography of English and American Literature Based on Greco-Roman Mythology.* Metuchen, NJ: Scarecrow Press, 1982.

Capps, Donald, Lewis Rambo, and Paul Ransohoff. *Psychology of Religion: A Guide to Information Sources.* Detroit, MI: Gale Research, 1976.

Carlyon, Richard. *A Guide to the Gods.* New York: Morrow, 1981.

Cavendish, Richard, and Trevor Ling. *Mythology: An Illustrated Encyclopedia.* New York: Marshall Cavendish, 1983.

Classics, Folklore, and Mythology in the Classroom. Focused Access to Selected Topics (FAST) Bibliography No. 38. Bloomington, IN: ERIC Clearinghouse on Reading and Communication Skills, 1989. ED 308548

Diehl, Katharine Smith. *Religions, Mythologies, Folklores: An Annotated Bibliography.* 2nd ed. Metuchen, NJ: Scarecrow Press, 1962.

Folk, Judith A. *Around the World Through Stories: An Annotated Bibliography of Folk Literature.* Honolulu, HI: Graduate School of Library Science, Hawaii University, 1988. ED 309779.

Kohn, Rita T. *Mythology for Young People: A Reference Guide.* New York: Garland Publishing, 1985.

Kulikowski, Mark. *A Bibliography of Slavic Mythology.* Columbus, OH: Slavica, 1989.

Lindow, John. *Scandinavian Mythology: An Annotated Bibliography.* New York: Garland Publishing, 1988.

Lozano, Eduardo. "Bibliography: Indian Religion and Mythology." *Latin American Indian Literatures Journal: A Review of American Indian Texts* 5, no. 2 (Fall 1989), pp. 84-94.

Maud, Ralph. *A Guide to B. C. Indian Myth and Legend: A Short History of Myth-Collecting and a Survey of Published Texts.* Vancouver, BC: Talonbooks, 1982.

Montgomery, Paula K. *Narrative Folklore: The Fable, Folk Tale, Legend, and Myth.* Rockville, MD: Montgomery County Public Schools, 1980. ED 188238.

Niles, Susan A. *South American Indian Narrative, Theoretical and Analytic Approaches: An Annotated Bibliography.* New York: Garland Publishing, 1981.

Peradotto, John. *Classical Mythology: An Annotated Bibliographical Survey.* Urbana, IL: American Philological Association, 1973.

Smith, Ron. *Mythologies of the World: A Guide to Sources.* Urbana, IL: National Council of Teachers of English, 1981.

Reference Books

Some references are never used in their entirety but serve the purpose of providing encyclopedic coverage of the topic. These sources provide reference to answer questions that students are likely to ask.

Barber, Richard W. *A Companion to World Mythology.* New York: Delacorte Press, 1979.

Baumgartner, Anne S. *Ye Gods! A Dictionary of the Gods.* Secaucus, NJ: Lyle Stuart, 1984.

Bell, Robert E. *Dictionary of Classical Mythology, Symbols, Attributes, and Associations.* Santa Barbara, CA: ABC-Clio, 1982.

———. *Place-Names in Classical Mythology: Greece.* Santa Barbara, CA: ABC-Clio, 1988.

Boswell, Fred, and Jeanetta Boswell. *What Men or Gods Are These? A Genealogical Approach to Classical Mythology.* Metuchen, NJ: Scarecrow Press, 1980.

Cotterell, Arthur. *A Dictionary of World Mythology.* New York: Putnam, 1982.

Daly, Kathleen. *Greek and Roman Mythology A to Z: A Young Reader's Companion.* New York: Facts on File, 1992.

Ellis, Peter Berresford. *A Dictionary of Irish Mythology.* Santa Barbara, CA: ABC-Clio, 1989.

Evans, Bergen Baldwin. *Dictionary of Mythology, Mainly Classical.* New York: Dell, 1970.

Feder, Lillian. *Crowell's Handbook of Classical Literature.* New York: Lippincott, 1964.

Frazer, Sir James George. *The Golden Bough.* New York: St. Martin's, 1969.

Gaster, Theodore. *The New Golden Bough.* New York: St. Martin's, 1975.

Grant, Michael, and John Hazel. *Gods and Mortals in Classical Mythology.* New York: Dorset, 1979.

Grimal, Pierre. *A Concise Dictionary of Classical Mythology.* Cambridge, MA: Basil Blackwell, 1990.

Hammond, N. G. L., and H. H. Scullard. *The Oxford Classical Dictionary.* New York: Clarendon/Oxford, 1970.

Hendricks, Rhoda A. *Mythologies of the World: A Concise Encyclopedia.* New York: McGraw-Hill, 1981.

Howatson, M. C. *The Oxford Companion to Classical Literature.* New York: Oxford University Press, 1989.

Jobes, Gertrude. *Dictionary of Mythology, Folklore, and Symbols.* Metuchen, NJ: Scarecrow Press, 1962.

Kravitz, David. *Who's Who in Greek and Roman Mythology.* New York: Clarkson N. Potter, 1976.

Lurker, Manfred, and G. L. Campbell. *Dictionary of Gods and Goddesses, Devils and Demons.* New York: Routledge, Chapman and Hall, 1987.

McDonald, Margaret Read. *The Folklore of World Holidays.* Detroit, MI: Gale Research, 1992.

McGowen, Tom. *Encyclopedia of Legendary Creatures.* Chicago: Rand McNally, 1981.

McHargue, Georgess. *The Impossible People: A History Natural and Unnatural of Beings Terrible and Wonderful*. New York: Holt, Rinehart and Winston, 1972.

Mercatante, Anthony S. *The Facts on File Encyclopedia of World Mythology and Legend*. New York: Facts on File, 1988.

————. *Who's Who in Egyptian Mythology*. New York: Clarkson N. Potter, 1978.

Monaghan, Patricia. *The Book of Goddesses and Heroines*. New York: Llewellyn, 1990.

Murray, Alexander S. *Who's Who in Mythology: Classic Guide to the Ancient World*. New York: Crescent Books, 1988.

Palmer, Robin. *A Dictionary of Mythical Places*. New York: Walck, 1975.

Schmidt, Joel. *Larousse Greek and Roman Mythology*. New York: A. S. Barnes, 1972.

Stapleton, Michael. *A Dictionary of Greek and Roman Mythology*. Denver, CO: Bell Publications, 1978.

Walker, Barbara G. *The Woman's Encyclopedia of Myths and Secrets*. New York: Harper and Row, 1983.

Zimmerman, J. E. *Dictionary of Classical Mythology*. New York: Harper and Row, 1964.

Teaching Sources

Teaching sources containing ideas about how others have presented the materials in the classroom serve as a fourth category of professional material. These articles and books allow the teacher or library media specialist to look at other educators' outlines, objectives, strategies, and assessments for motivating students to read mythology.

Anderson, Mary Ann. "Social Studies: Lessons from Mount Olympus." *Teacher* 94, no. 4 (December 1976), pp. 57-58.

Comm, Lisabeth. "Experiencing Mythology and the Bible: Reading, Writing, Looking, and Dancing." *English Journal* 78, no. 7 (November 1989), pp. 34-39.

Davidson, Josephine. *Teaching and Dramatizing Greek Myths*. Englewood, CO: Libraries Unlimited, 1989.

Olson, Paul A. *The Uses of Myth: Pages Relating to the Anglo-American Seminar on the Teaching of English at Dartmouth College, New Hampshire, 1966*. Urbana, IL: National Council of Teachers of English, 1968.

Ring, Diane M. *Hindu Mythology: Gods, Goddesses and Values*. Washington, DC: Center for International Education, United States Educational Foundation in India, 1990. ED 329506

Wolverton, Robert E. *An Outline of Classical Mythology*. Totowa, NJ: Littlefield, Adams, 1971.

Periodicals

Although myths are among the oldest forms of narrative, periodicals continue to provide new ways of looking at this form. Browsing such periodicals helps keep one up-to-date on current studies and investigations.

Associations

Many metropolitan areas support associations of individuals who are interested in mythology and folklore. Consult local directories to find gatherings of experts.

Activity: Studying Mythology with Puppets and Marionettes

Marionettes are often considered difficult to make with large groups. Another option would be shadow puppets, as those found in Bali, India, China, Japan, and Indonesia (Java). There are many kinds of rod and shadow puppets. In India, Putliwala puppeteers spend up to half a day retelling myths and legends from the Ramayana with wooden puppets. The Indonesian Wjang-Kelitik is a marionette/puppet used to retell traditional stories while the Waynag Kulit uses leather to make shadow puppets on rods. Other groups in Indonesia have still more variations of shadow or rod puppets. Puppet shows are part of religious festivals and continue for hours into the night. These examples and others may be shown to dramatic effect in videocassettes such as the *Ring of Fire* (Mystic Video).

This activity can be successfully introduced with a sample puppet show performed by the teacher and library media specialist. Set up an overhead projector and prepare several flat shadow puppets to accompany a simple myth, perhaps from one of the Asian countries. Introduce students to a modern, modified method of performance with shadow puppets by laying flat puppets on the overhead projector to project on a screen. Several puppets in the style of the Javanese might be shared with students. Viewers may sit on the same side of the screen as the performers to watch them work. Usually viewers sit on the side of the screen opposite the performers to view the play in shadow. In Indonesia, a large screen is set up and an oil lamp often provides the lighting. The puppets are operated between the lamp and the screen so that puppet shadows are cast on the screen. Puppets are usually flat and mounted on rods. Often the rods are attached to the puppeteer's hands but may also be held by other moving body parts.

Explain that the students will work in small groups to develop an original shadow puppet play in the style of the Javanese. Instruct students to search for stories from Indonesia, select one, and make puppets to perform the story. In the process, the students will find information about the music of the Javanese, the people themselves, as well as shadow puppetry.

Group the students, four children to a group. Assign them the task of doing the appropriate research and prepare the shadow puppet plays. The library media specialist may introduce a quick research strategy:

Suggested Research Method

1. Check for pictures and information about Indonesia or Java in encyclopedias and geography materials. How do the Javanese enjoy shadow puppets as a form of entertainment?
2. Use the card or automated catalog and encyclopedias to locate information about shadow puppets. How are the puppets made and used?
3. Locate Indonesian stories.

Assist groups of students in dividing the research work, collecting information, and choosing an appropriate story to present as a shadow play. They will use an overhead projector instead of a large screen and oil lamp. The next step will be to decide on number of puppets needed as well as minimum transparency background. Students may examine intricate examples of shadow puppets illustrated in encyclopedias as a guide to the artistic styles. Puppets may be made and decorated. The group members should choose if a narrator will tell the story or if group members will divide the responsibility. Practice is necessary. When the students are ready, they may present their Javanese shadow plays to the class.

As a follow-up activity, ask students to locate information about the shadow puppets used in China, Japan, Iraq, and other Middle Eastern countries in order to compare the kinds of plays and stories that come from each country, the forms of the puppets, and the methods of presentation. Research might lead to the production of a videotaped series of stories told by student groups. In the process, students may locate stories that are suitable for shadow puppets. Students will also discover the difficulty of locating Indonesian myths.

Student Sources

The following books and materials on myths are recommended for use with young adults. There are many picture books that have been excluded from this list, although such books could be useful as motivators. Every effort has been made to include mythology representing varied racial, ethnic, and cultural groups. Christian religious materials have been limited to stories from the Bible about creation and the great flood. Given that a simple story in one cultural group has religious significance to another, thought and sensitivity will be needed to select appropriate myths. If Greek myths are used, an effort should be made to help students understand the significance of the stories in terms of purpose of the telling. Older titles can be found in well-established library media collections. IL indicates the general interest level of the material, and RL indicates the Fry estimated reading level of the material.

Print

Alpers, Anthony. *Legends of the South Seas: The World of the Polynesians Seen Through Their Myths and Legends, Poetry, and Art.* New York: T. Y. Crowell, 1970. IL: 6-8.

Anderson, Johannes E. *Myths and Legends of the Polynesians.* Rutland, VT: C. E. Tuttle, 1969. IL: 6-8.

Avery, Catherine B. *The New Century Handbook of Greek Mythology and Legend.* New York: Meredith Corporation, 1962. IL: 6-8.

Baily, John, Kenneth McLeish, and David Spearman. *Gods and Men: Myths and Legends from the World's Religions.* New York: Oxford University Press, 1981. IL: 5-8.

Baker, Betty. *At the Center of the World; Based on Papago and Pima Myths.* New York: Macmillan, 1973. IL: 4-7.

Barth, Edna. *Cupid and Psyche, A Love Story.* New York: Seabury Press, 1976. IL: 4-7.

Baylor, Byrd. *Way To Start the Day.* New York: Scribner's, 1978. IL: 3-6; RL: 5.

Beckwith, Martha Warren. *Hawaiian Mythology.* Honolulu, HI: University of Hawaii Press, 1977. IL: 5-8.

Benson, Sally. *Stories of the Gods and Heroes.* New York: Dell, 1979. IL: 5-9.

Bierhorst, John. *Black Rainbow: Legends of the Incas and Myths of Ancient Peru.* New York: Farrar, Straus and Giroux, 1976. IL: 7-9.

————. *The Hungry Woman: Myths and Legends of the Aztecs.* New York: Morrow, 1984. IL: 7-9.

————. *The Mythology of Mexico and Central America.* New York: Morrow, 1990. IL: 7-9.

————. *Mythology of South America.* New York: Morrow, 1988. IL: 7-9.

————. *The Red Swan: Myths and Tales of the American Indians.* New York: Farrar, Straus and Giroux, 1976. IL: 7-9.

Bishop, Morris. *A Classical Storybook.* Ithaca, NY: Cornell University Press, 1970. IL: 7-9.

Branston, Brian. *Gods and Heroes from Viking Mythology*. New York: Schocken Books, 1982. IL: 5-9+.

———. *Gods of the North*. New York: Thames and Hudson, 1980. IL: 5-9.

Brown, Hanbury. *Man and the Stars*. New York: Oxford University Press, 1978. IL: 7-9.

Brown, Marcia. *Backbone of the King*. Honolulu, HI: University of Hawaii Press, 1984. IL: 4-7.

Bulfinch, Thomas. *Bulfinch's Mythology. The Age of Fable. The Age of Chivalry. Legends of Charlemagne*. New York: Viking, 1979. IL: 7-9+.

———. *Myths of Greece and Rome*. New York: Penguin, 1981. IL: 5-9.

Burland, Cottie Arthur. *Feathered Serpent and Smoking Mirror: The Gods and Cultures of Ancient Mexico*. New York: Putnam, 1975. IL: 5-8.

Carpenter, Frances. *People from the Sky: Ainu Tales from Northern Japan*. Garden City, NY: Doubleday, 1972. IL: 4-7.

Chatterjee, Debjani. *The Elephant-Headed God: And Other Hindu Tales*. New York: Oxford University Press, 1993. IL: 4-6.

Church, Alfred J. *The Iliad and the Odyssey of Homer*. New York: Macmillan, 1964. IL: 5-8.

Coffer, William E. *Where Is the Eagle?* New York: Van Nostrand Reinhold, 1981. IL: 8-9+.

Colum, Padraic. *The Children of Odin: Book of Northern Myths*. New York: Macmillan, 1984. IL: 5-8; RL: 6.

———. *The Children's Homer: The Adventures of Odysseus and the Tale of Troy*. New York: Macmillan, 1982. IL: 5-8.

———. *The Golden Fleece and the Heroes Who Lived Before Achilles*. New York: Macmillan, 1983. IL: 5-8.

———. *Myths of the World*. New York: Grosset and Dunlap, 1972. IL: 7-9+.

Coolidge, Olivia. *Greek Myths*. Boston: Houghton Mifflin, 1949. IL: 7-9; RL: 9.

———. *Legends of the North*. Boston: Houghton Mifflin, 1951. IL: 5-8.

Coomaraswamy, Ananda K., and Sr. Nivedita. *Myths of the Hindus and Buddhists*. New York: Dover. IL: 6-9+.

Courlander, Harold. *Tales of Yoruba Gods and Heroes*. New York: Crown, 1972. IL: 5-8.

Crossley-Holland, Kevin. *Axe-Age, Wolf-Age: A Selection of Norse Myths*. New York: Andre Deutsch, 1987. IL: 7-9.

———. *The Norse Myths*. New York: Pantheon, 1980. IL: 7-9+; RL: 8.

Dasent, George W. *The Story of Burnt Njal*. Atlanta, GA: Bibliotheca Press, 1971. IL: 7-9+.

D'Aulaire, Ingri, and Edgar Parin D'Aulaire. *Book of Greek Myths*. Garden City, NY: Doubleday, 1980. IL: 4-7; RL: 7.

Dowrick, Stephanie. *Land of Zeus: The Greek Myths Retold by Geographical Place of Origin*. Garden City, NY: Doubleday, 1976. IL: 6-8.

Dowson, John. *A Classical Dictionary of Hindu Mythology and Religion.* Mystic, CT: Lawrence Verry, 1973. IL: 5-9+.

Eliade, Mircea. *Gods, Goddesses and Myths of Creation: A Thematic Source Book of the History of Religions.* New York: Harper and Row, 1974, IL: 7-9+.

Emerson, Nathaniel B. *Pele and Hiiaka: A Myth from Hawaii.* Rutland, VT: Tuttle, 1978. IL: 7-9.

Evslin, Bernard. *The Cyclops.* New York: Chelsea House, 1987. IL: 7-9; RL: 6.

———. *The Furies.* New York: Chelsea House, 1989. IL: 6-8; RL: 6.

———. *The Hydra.* New York: Chelsea House, 1989. IL: 6-8; RL: 6.

———. *The Medusa.* New York: Chelsea House, 1989. IL: 6-8; RL: 6.

———. *The Minotaur.* New York: Chelsea House, 1989. IL: 6-8; RL: 6.

———. *The Nemean Lion.* New York: Chelsea House, 1990. IL: 6-8; RL: 6.

———. *The Sphinx.* New York: Chelsea House, 1990. IL: 6-8; RL: 6.

Farady, Lucy Winifred. *The Edda.* New York: AMS Press, 1972. IL: 7-9+.

Farmer, Penelope. *Beginnings: Creation Myths of the World.* New York: Atheneum, 1978. IL: 7-9.

———. *Daedalus and Icarus.* New York: Harcourt Brace Jovanovich, 1971. IL: 5-7.

Feldman, Susan. *African Myths and Tales.* New York: Dell, 1963. IL: 7-8.

Feldman, Susan. *The Storytelling Stone: Myths and Tales of the American Indians.* New York: Dell, 1971. IL: 7-9.

Fisher, Leonard Everett. *Olympians: Great Gods and Goddesses of Ancient Greece.* New York: Holiday House, 1984. IL: 5-8; RL: 7.

Gaer, Joseph. *The Adventures of Rama.* Boston: Little, Brown, 1954. IL: 5-8.

Garfield, Leon, and Edward Blishen. *The God Beneath the Sea: A Recreation of the Greek Legends.* New York: Pantheon Press, 1971. IL: 7-9.

———. *The Golden Shadow: A Recreation of the Greek Legends.* New York: Pantheon, 1973. IL: 7-9.

Gates, Doris. *A Fair Wind for Troy.* New York: Viking Press, 1976. IL: 7-9.

———. *The Golden God: Apollo.* New York: Puffin Books, 1983. IL: 4-7.

———. *Lord of the Sky: Zeus.* New York: Puffin Books, 1982. IL: 4-7.

———. *Mightiest of Mortals: Heracles.* New York: Viking, 1975. IL: 5-7.

———. *Two Queens of Heaven: Aphrodite and Demeter.* New York: Puffin Books, 1983. IL: 7-9.

———. *The Warrior Goddess: Athena.* New York: Puffin Books, 1982. IL: 5-7.

Gibson, Michael. *Gods, Men and Monsters from the Greek Myths.* New York: Schocken Books, 1982. IL: 4-7.

Gifford, Douglas. *Warriors, Gods and Spirits from Central and South American Mythology.* New York: Schocken Books, 1983. IL: 7-9.

Gimbutas, Marija. *The Goddesses and Gods of Old Europe 6500-3500 BC; Cult Images.* Berkeley, CA: University of California Press, 1982. IL: 6-8+.

Gottlieb, Gerald. *The Adventures of Ulysses.* Hamden, CT: Linnet Books, 1988. IL: 7-9.

Grant, Michael. *Myths of the Greeks and Romans.* New York: New American Library, 1962. IL: 7-9.

Graves, Robert. *The Greek Myths, Vols. 1 and 2.* New York: Penguin, 1960. IL: 7-9+.

Graves, Robert, and Raphael Patai. *Hebrew Myths: The Book of Genesis.* New York: McGraw-Hill, 1966. IL: 7-9+.

Gray, J. E. B. *India's Tales and Legends.* New York: Oxford University Press, 1979. IL: 5-9.

Green, Roger Lancelyn. *A Book of Myths.* New York: Dutton, 1965. IL: 5-9+.

———. *Heroes of Greece and Troy, Retold from the Ancient Authors.* London: Bodley Head, 1973. IL: 7-9.

———. *Tales of Ancient Egypt.* New York: Penguin, 1970. IL: 4-7.

Hamilton, Edith. *The Greek Way.* New York: Norton, 1948. IL: 7-9+.

———. *Mythology.* New York: New American Library, 1940. IL: 7-9+. RL: 11.

Hamilton, Virginia. *The Dark Way: Stories from the Spirit World.* New York: Harcourt Brace Jovanovich, 1990. IL: 7-9.

———. *In the Beginning: Creation Stories from Around the World.* New York: Harcourt Brace Jovanovich, 1988. IL: 5-8; RL: 5.

Harris, Geraldine. *Gods and Pharaohs from Egyptian Mythology.* New York: Schocken Books, 1983. IL: 5-8.

Hawthorne, Nathaniel. *Tanglewood Tales.* New York: Airmont, 1968. IL: 7-9.

Helfman, Elizabeth S. *Maypoles and Wood Demons: The Meaning of Trees.* New York: Seabury Press, 1972. IL: 4-7.

Highwater, Jamake. *Many Smokes, Many Moons: A Chronology of American Indian History through Indian Art.* New York: Lippincott, 1978. IL: 5-9.

Hinnels, John R. *Persian Mythology.* London: P. Hamlyn Books, 1973. IL: 5-8.

Hodges, Margaret. *Baldur and the Mistletoe.* Boston: Little, Brown, 1975. IL: 5-8.

———. *The Golden Deer.* New York: Scribner's, 1992. IL: 3-6.

———. *The Other World: Myths of the Celts.* New York: Farrar, Straus and Giroux, 1973. IL: 5-8.

Ions, Veronica. *Egyptian Mythology.* New York: P. Hamlyn Books, 1983. IL: 5-8.

———. *Indian Mythology.* New York: P. Hamlyn Books, 1967. IL: 5-8.

———. *World's Mythology.* New York: P. Hamlyn Books, 1974. IL: 7-9+.

Jagendorf, Moritz Adolph. *Stories and Lore of the Zodiac.* New York: Vanguard Press, 1977. IL: 5-8.

Judson, Katerine Berry. *Myths and Legends of the Pacific Northwest.* Seattle, WA: Shorey Publications, 1982. IL: 7-9.

Katz, Jane B. *This Song Remembers: Self-Portraits of Native Americans in the Arts.* Boston: Houghton Mifflin, 1980. IL: 6-9.

Kerven, Rosalind. *The Slaying of the Dragon: Tales of the Hindu Gods.* New York: Andre Deutsch, 1987. IL: 7-9.

Knappert, Jan. *Kings, Gods and Spirits from African Mythology.* New York: Schocken Books, 1986. IL: 7-9.

————. *Myths and Legends of the Congo*. Nairobi: Heinemann Educational, 1971. IL: 5-8.

Kroeber, A. L. *Yurok Myths*. Berkeley, CA: University of California Press, 1976. IL: 8-9+.

Lang, Andrew. *The Adventures of Odysseus*. New York: Dutton, 1962. IL: 5-8.

Lattimore, Deborah Nourse. *Why There Is No Arguing in Heaven: A Mayan Myth*. New York: HarperCollins, 1989. IL: 4-6; RL: 4.

LaVine, Sigmund A. *The Ghosts the Indians Feared*. New York: Dodd, Mead, 1975. IL: 7-9.

Lewis, Richard. *All of You Was Singing*. New York: Macmillan, 1991. IL: 6-9; RL: 4.

Lines, Kathleen. *The Faber Book of Greek Legends*. Salem, NH: Faber, 1973. IL: 5-8.

Low, Alice. *Macmillan Book of Greek Gods and Heroes*. New York: Macmillan, 1985. IL: 5-8; RL: 8.

Mandelbaum, Allen. *The Odyssey of Homer; A New Verse Translation by Allen Mandelbaum*. Berkeley, CA: University of California Press, 1990. IL: 8-9+.

Marriott, Alice Lee. *American Indian Mythology*. New York: Thomas Y. Crowell, 1972. IL: 6-9.

————. *Plains Indian Mythology*. New York: Thomas Y. Crowell, 1975. IL: 7-9.

McAlpine, Helen, and William McAlpine. *Japanese Tales and Legends*. New York: Oxford University Press, 1980. IL: 4-8.

Melzack, Ronald. *The Day Tuk Became a Hunter and Other Eskimo Stories*. Boston: Little, Brown, 1968. IL: 4-7.

————. *Raven, Creator of the World*. Boston: Little, Brown, 1970. IL: 5-8.

Meyer, Marianna. *Iduna and the Magic Apples*. New York: Macmillan, 1988. IL: 5-8; RL: 6.

Miles, Patricia. *The Gods in Winter*. New York: Dutton, 1978. IL: 5-8.

Monroe, Jean Guard, and Ray A. Williamson. *First Houses: Native American Homes and Sacred Structures*. Boston: Houghton Mifflin, 1993. IL: 7-9.

Morford, Mark P. O., and Robert J. Lenardon. *Classical Mythology*. New York: McKay, 1977. IL: 7-9.

Mountford, C. P. *The First Sunrise: Australian Aboriginal Myths*. London: Robert Hale, 1972. IL: 7-9+.

Naravane, V. S. *A Dictionary of Indian Mythology*. New York: Advent, 1984. IL: 5-8.

Nelson, Ralph. *Popol Vuh: The Great Mythological Book of the Ancient Maya*. Boston: Houghton Mifflin, 1976. IL: 7-9.

O'Flaherty, Wendy Doniger. *Hindu Myths: A Sourcebook*. New York: Penguin, 1975. IL: 7-9+.

Oppenheim, Shulamith Levy. *Iblis: An Islamic Tale*. New York: Harcourt Brace Jovanovich, 1994. IL: 3-6.

Osborne, Mary Pope. *Favorite Greek Myths*. New York: Scholastic, 1988. IL: 5-8; RL: 6.

Picard, Barbara Leonie. *Iliad of Homer.* New York: Oxford University Press, 1980. IL: 5-8.

Picard, Barbara Leonie. *The Story of Rama and Sita.* London: Harrap, 1960. IL: 5-7.

Piggott, Juliet. *Japanese Mythology.* New York: Peter Bedrick Books, 1983. IL: 5-9+.

Pinsent, John. *Greek Mythology.* New York: Peter Bedrick Books, 1983. IL: 6-9+.

Proddow, Penelope. *Demeter and Persephone: Homeric Hymn Number Two.* Garden City, NY: Doubleday, 1972. IL: 5-8.

————. *Hermes, Lord of Robbers: Homeric Hymn Number Four.* Garden City, NY: Doubleday, 1971. IL: 5-8.

Reed, A. W. *Aboriginal Myths: Tales of the Dreamtime.* Rutland, VT: C. E. Tuttle, 1979. IL: 5-8.

————. *Maori Myth: The Supernatural World of the Maori.* Rutland, VT: C. E. Tuttle, 1977. IL: 5-9.

————. *Myths and Legends of Australia.* New York: Taplinger Publishing Co., 1973. IL: 5-8.

Reeves, James. *The Voyage of Odysseus: Homer's Odyssey.* New York: Bedrick/Blackie, 1986. IL: 7-9.

Rieu, Emil V. *The Odyssey.* New York: Greenwich House, 1982. IL: 7-9+.

————. *Iliad.* New York: Penguin, 1950. IL: 7-9+.

Rose, H. J. *A Handbook of Mythology.* New York: Dutton, 1959. IL: 5-8.

Ross, Anne. *Druids, Gods and Heroes from Celtic Mythology.* New York: Schocken Books, 1986. IL: 7-9.

Russell, William F. *Classic Myths to Read Aloud.* New York: Crown, 1989. IL: 3-7; RL: 8.

Saunders, Tao Tao Liu. *Dragons, Gods and Spirits from Chinese Mythology.* New York: Schocken Books, 1983. IL: 6-9.

Schwab, Gustav. *Gods and Heroes: Myths and Epics of Ancient Greece.* New York: Random House, 1977. IL: 6-9+.

Seed, Jenny. *The Bushman's Dream: African Tales of the Creation.* Scarsdale, NY: Bradbury Press, 1975. IL: 5-8.

Seeger, Elizabeth. *The Ramayana.* New York: William R. Scott, 1969. IL: 5-9+

Serraillier, Ian. *The Clashing Rocks: The Story of the Argo.* New York: Walck, 1964. IL: 5-8.

————. *Fall from the Sky: The Story of Daedalus.* New York: Walck, 1966. IL: 5-8.

————. *Gorgon's Head: The Story of Perseus.* New York: Walck, 1962. IL: 5-8.

The Seven Days of Creation. New York: Holiday House, 1981. IL: 4-9+.

Severin, Tom. *The Ulysses Voyage: Sea Search for the Odyssey.* New York: Dutton, 1987. IL: 8-9+.

Seymour, Tryntje Van Ness. *The Gift of Changing Woman.* New York: Henry Holt, 1993. IL: 4-6.

Skinner, Charles M. *Myths and Legends of Flowers, Trees, Fruits and Plants in All Ages and in All Climes.* New York: Gordon Press, 1976. IL: 5-8.

Stone, Merlin. *Ancient Mirrors of Womanhood: A Treasury of Goddesses and Heroine Lore from Around the World.* Boston: Beacon Press, 1984. IL: 7-9+.

Sun Bear and Wabun. *The Medicine Wheel: Earth Astrology.* Englewood Cliffs, NJ: Prentice-Hall, 1980. IL: 8-9+.

Switzer, Ellen, and Costas. *Greek Myths: Gods, Heroes, and Monsters; Their Sources, Their Stories and Their Meanings.* New York: Atheneum, 1988. IL: 7-9.

Synge, Ursula. *Land of the Heroes: A Retelling of the Kalevala.* New York: Atheneum, 1978. IL: 5-8.

Thompson, Vivian Lauback. *Hawaiian Myths of Earth, Sea, and Sky.* New York: Holiday House, 1966. IL: 4-7.

———. *Hawaiian Tales of Heroes and Champions.* New York: Holiday House, 1971. IL: 4-7.

Traven, B. *The Creation of the Sun and the Moon.* Westport, CT: Lawrence Hill and Co., 1977. IL: 6-8.

Tyler, Hamilton A. *Pueblo Animals and Myths.* Norman, OK: University of Oklahoma, 1975. IL: 7-9+.

———. *Pueblo Birds and Myths.* Norman, OK: University of Oklahoma Press, 1979. IL: 7-9+.

———. *Pueblo Gods and Myths.* Norman, OK: University of Oklahoma, 1984. IL: 7-9+.

Usher, Kerry. *Heroes, Gods and Emperors from Roman Mythology.* New York: Schocken Books, 1984. IL: 5-8.

Van Over, Raymond. *Sun Songs: Creation Myths from Around the World.* New York: Mentor Books, 1980. IL: 7-9.

Virgil. *The Aeneid.* Translated by Robert Fitzgerald. Random House, 1983. IL: 8-9+.

Warner, Elizabeth. *Heroes, Monsters and Other Worlds from Russian Mythology.* New York: Schocken Books, 1985. IL: 7-9.

White, Anne Terry. *The Golden Treasury of Myths and Legends.* Racine, WI: Golden Books, 1959. IL: 5-8.

Wolkstein, Diane, and Samuel Noah Kramer. *Inana: Queen of Heaven and Earth. Her Stories and Hymns from Sumer.* New York: Harper and Row, 1983. IL: 7-9+.

Wood, Nancy C. *Gold of the Gods.* Chicago: Childrens Press, 1982. IL: 5-8.

Nonprint

Ancient Myths and Legends. Chicago: Society for Visual Education, 1989. 4 sound filmstrips.

Colum, Padraic. *The Children of Odin: The Book of Northern Myths.* Read by Keir Dullen. New York: Caedmon TC 1471. 1 record.

———. *The Twelve Labors of Heracles and Other Adventures.* Read by Anthony Quayle. New York: Caedmon CDL5 1256. 1 audiocassette.

Flight of Icarus. Van Nuys, CA: ACI, 1974. 6 min. One 16mm film. Adapted from Gerald McDermott's *Sun Flight.* IFF, 1966.

Great Myths of Greece. Chicago: EBEC, 1972. 4 sound filmstrips.

The Greek Myths. Part I, Myth as Fiction, History, and Ritual. Chicago: EBEC, 1971. 25 min. One 16mm film.

The Greek Myths. Part II, Myth as Science, Religion, and Drama. Chicago: EBEC, 1971. 25 min. One 16mm film.

The Greek Myths: A Treasury. Volumes 1-5. New York: CMS, 1978. 5 records.

The Greeks, Part 3: Heroes and Men. Princeton, NJ: Films for the Humanities, 1980. 52 min. 1 videocassette.

Hawthorne, Nathaniel. *Tanglewood Tales.* Read by Anthony Quayle. New York: Caedmon TC 1290/TC 1291, 1969. 2 records.

Icarus and Daedalus. New York: Sterling, 1963. 6 min. One 16mm film.

Jason and the Argonauts. Pasadena, CA: Barr Films, 1988. 20 min. One 16mm film.

Jason and the Argonauts. New York: Time-Life, 1964. 103 min. One 16mm film.

McDermot, Gerald. *Arrow to the Sun.* Chicago: Texture Films, 1973. 12 min. One 16mm film.

———. *Sun Flight.* Old Greenwich, CT: Listening Library JFS200, 1984. 7 min. 1 sound cassette.

Millennium: Tribal Wisdom and the Modern World. Inventing Reality. New York: PBS/Biniman, 1992. 60 min. 1 videotape.

Myth of the Pharaohs. Van Nuys, CA: ACI, 1971. 13 min. One 16mm film.

Mythology of Greece and Rome. New York: BFA, 1968. 16 min. One 16 mm film.

Myths and Legends of Ancient Greece. Stamford, CT: Educational Dimensions, 1982. 4 sound filmstrips.

Myths of Greece and Rome. Chicago: Society for Visual Education, 1978. 4 sound filmstrips.

Narcissus. Chicago: Films Incorporated, 1975. 6 min. One 16mm film.

North American Indian Legends. New York: BFA, 1973. 21 min. One 16mm film.

Orpheus and Eurydice. New York: Sterling. 10 min. One 16mm film.

The Perilous Voyage: Homer's Odyssey. Princeton, NJ: Films for the Humanities, 1989. 15 min each. 6 videotapes.

Popol Vuh: The Creation Myth of the Maya. Berkeley, CA: University of California Extension Media Center, 1987. 29 min. One 16mm film.

Prometheus. Pasadena, CA: Barr Films. 18 min. One 16mm film.

Quest. Chicago: Films Incorporated, 1971. 18 min. One 16 mm film.

Roughsey, Dick. *Giant Devil Dingo.* Weston, CT: Weston Woods. 10 min. 1 videocassette.

Theseus and the Labyrinth. New York: Phoenix, Barr Films and Video, 1970. 20 min. One 16mm film.

Theseus and the Minotaur. Los Angeles, CA: Classroom Film Distributors, 1954. 15 min. One 16mm film.

Timeless Tales: Myths of Ancient Greece. Hawthorne, NJ: January Productions, 1982. 5 sound filmstrips.

Why the Sun and Moon Live in the Sky. Van Nuys, CA: AIMS Media, 1971. 11 min. One 16mm film.

World Myths and Folktales. Chicago: American School Publishers, 1974. 8 sound filmstrips.

The World Tree: A Scandinavian Creation Myth. Chicago: International Film Bureau, 1977. 10 min. One 16mm film.

Professional Sources

Print

Arrasjid, Dorine. "Shadow Puppets." *School Arts* 78, no. 5 (January 1979), pp. 20-22.

Bailey, Vanessa. *Shadow Theater: Games and Projects.* New York, Gloucester Press, 1991.

Batchelder, Marjorie. *Rod Puppets and the Human Theater.* Columbus, OH: Ohio State University Press, 1947.

Binyon, Helen. *Puppetry Today: Designing and Making Marionettes, Hand Puppets, Rod Puppets, and Shadow Puppets.* New York: Watson-Guptill, 1966.

Blackham, Olive. *Shadow Puppets.* New York: Harper, 1960.

Chin, Chen-An. *The Mainstay of the Chinese Shadow Show: The Lanchou Shadow Show.* Taipei, Taiwan, Republic of China: Student Book Co., 1993.

Cochrane, Louise. *Shadow Puppets In Color.* Boston: Plays, 1972.

Covarrubias, Miguel. "The Shadow Play in Bali and Java." *Theater Arts* 20 (August 1936), pp. 629-35.

Crothers, J. Francis. *The Puppeteer's Library Guide: The Bibliographic Index to the Literature of the World Puppet Theatre. Volume I: The Historical Background of Puppetry and Its Related Fields.* Metuchen, NJ: Scarecrow Press, 1971.

Damais, L. C. "Shadow Theatre in Java and Bali." *World Theater* 14 (September 1965), pp. 450-95.

Davies, Darlene Gould. "Hand, Finger, and Shadow . . . The Wonderful World of Puppets." *Perspectives for Teachers of the Hearing Impaired* 3, no. 5 (May-June 1985), pp. 14-16.

Devereaux, Kent, and Deborah Zick. *Wayang Purwa: An American Adaptation of a Javanese Shadow Play.* Calcutta, India: Writers Workshop, 1989.

Frazier, Nancy. *Imagination: At Play With Puppets and Creative Drama.* Austin, TX: Nancy Renfro Studios, 1987.

Hobart, Angela. *Balinese Shadow Play Figures: Their Social and Ritual Significance.* London: British Museum, Dept. of Ethnography, 1985.

———. *Dancing Shadows of Bali: Theatre and Myth.* New York: KPI, 1987.

Joyce, Hope. *Me and My Shadows: 14 Royalty-Free Shadow Puppet Plays for Use on the Overhead Projector.* San Diego: Joy-Co Press, 1981.

Keeler, Ward, and Kathy Foley. *Puppet Theater of the Javanese and Puppet Theatre of the Sundanese*. New York: Festival of Indonesia Foundation, 1991.

Larson, Janice. "Shadow Puppets." *Reading Teacher* 44, no. 2 (October 1990), pp. 184.

Levy, Mark. "Wayang Kulit." *High Performance* 12, no. 2 (Summer 1989), p. 38.

Lynch-Watson, Janet. *The Shadow Puppet Book*. New York: Sterling Publishing, 1980.

Lysloff, Rene T.A. "A Wrinkle in Time: The Shadow Puppet Theatre of Banyumas (West Central Java)." *Asian Theatre Journal* 10, no. 1 (Spring 1993), p. 49.

McNeil, Jacqueline. "Shadows That Light Up the Classroom." *Teacher* 96, no. 5 (January 1981), pp. 42-44.

Moloney, Joan. *Making Puppets and Puppet Theatres*. New York: Fell, 1973.

Myrsiades, Linda S., and Kostas Myrsiades. *Karagiozis: Culture and Comedy in Greek Puppet Theater*. Lexington, KY: University Press of Kentucky, 1992.

Politi, Leo. *Mr. Fong's Toy Shop*. New York: Scribner's, 1978.

Reiniger, Lotte. *Shadow Theatre and Shadow Films*. London: Batsford, 1970.

Ross, Laura. *Scrap Puppets: How to Make and Move Them*. New York: Holt, Rinehart and Winston, 1978.

Ross, Laura, and Frank Ross, Jr. *Finger Puppets: Easy to Make, Fun to Use*. New York: Lothrop, Lee and Shepard, 1971.

Sierra, Judy. *Fantastic Theater: Puppets and Plays for Young Performers and Young Audiences*. New York: H. W. Wilson, 1991.

Sievert, Bob. "Big Foot in the Bronx—Shadow Puppets." *Teachers and Writers* 9, no. 1 (February 1977), pp. 26-29.

Sweeney, Amin. *Malay Shadow Puppets: The Wayang Siam of Kelantan*. London: British Museum, 1980.

Sylvester, Roland. "Shadow Puppetry in a Design Class." *School Arts* 69, no. 10 (June 1970), pp. 12-14.

Taylor, Loren E. *Puppetry, Marionettes and Shadow Plays*. Minneapolis, MN: Burgess Publishing, 1965.

VanSchuyver, Jan M. "The Magic of Puppetry: Shadow Puppets Make It Easy." *Top of the News* 42, no. 4 (Summer 1986), pp. 357-64.

Wiesner, William. *Hansel and Gretel: A Shadow Puppet Picture Book*. New York: Seabury Press, 1971.

Wright, John. *Rod, Shadow, and Glove: Puppets from the Little Angel Theatre*. London: R. Hale, 1986.

Young, Ed. *The Rooster's Horns: A Chinese Puppet Play To Make and Perform*. New York : Collins/World/U.S. Committee for UNICEF, 1978.

Nonprint

Aesop's Fables. Austin, TX: Nancy Renfro Studios, 1987. 1 kit.

Chinese Shadow Play. New York: China Film Enterprise of America/Pictura Films Co., 1947. 11 min. One 16mm film.

Chinese Folk Arts: China Art Film. Kwang Hwa Mass Communications, 1976. 23 min. 1 videocassette.

Chinese Shadow Plays. New York: New York State Department of Education and The Performing Arts Program of the Asia Society. 30 min. 1 videocassette.

Ring of Fire. Mantauk, NY: Mystic Fire Video, 1989. 55 min. each. 4 videocassettes.

Shadow Play of Bali. Berkeley, CA: University of California Extension Media Center. 6 min. 1 videocassette.

Shadow Puppet Theater of Java. Los Angeles, CA: Baylis-Glascock, 1970. 22 min. 1 videocassette.

Wayang Kulit: The Shadow Puppet Theater of Java. Los Angeles, CA: Baylis Glascock Films, 1970. 22 min. 1 videocassette.

Periodicals

International Yearbook of Puppetry. Pasadena, CA: Puppeteers of America.

A Propos. Semi-annual. Ultima-U.S.A. American Center of the Union Internationale de la Marionettes, Hyde Park, NY 12538

Puppetry Journal. Quarterly. Puppeteers of America, 5 Cricklewood Path, Pasadena, CA 91107.

Associations

Puppeteers of America
5 Cricklewood Path
Pasadena, CA 91107
Publishes: Annual Yearbook and *Puppetry Journal*

Ultima-U.S.A., American Center of the Union Internationale de la
    Marionette
Browning Road
Hyde Park, NY 12538
914-266-5953
Publishes: *A Propos*

3

Expository Writing

INTRODUCTION

E xposition or expository writing explains the nature of an idea, an object, or a theme. Although it is a distinct literary form, it relies on other forms of writing (Figure 3). It occupies a great deal of space in most libraries and is often considered "nonfiction" because of the factual information supplied. While nonfiction includes all forms of writing, exposition as nonfiction dominates all other forms in materials that are written to inform and explain.

What are the characteristics of expository writing? While it clarifies and gives factual information, topics are not necessarily about real persons, places, or events. Also the author sometimes presents a point of view which may or may not be his or her own, and that point of view may shift. The audience is addressed as if it were ready to receive the information being offered in the communication. The author usually shows understanding of the audience's prior knowledge of the subject. This is an element of the author's style, as he or she acknowledges a consciousness of the audience in terms of the language used, the complexity of sentences and paragraphs, and the organizational pattern. Ideas are arranged in patterns that show a progression of thought and interrelationship of ideas.

When the reader begins to read an expository piece, he or she expects to find concepts and summaries. Generalized information is supported by details. The reading level varies within the text because authors often vary the use of simple and complex sentences. Topic sentences that summarize are likely to be either found at the beginning, in the middle, or at the end of paragraphs, or sometimes are inferred.

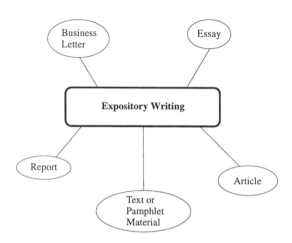

Figure 3. Expository Forms

The reader will find common relationship patterns in expository writing. An author defines and discusses a complex topic for the reader. A main idea or concept is presented and details are provided to give the idea meaning. The author sometimes illustrates an idea with examples, and at other times choose to provide analysis of information in categorized areas. Information may be arranged sequentially or chronologically when time is an underlying factor.

When the author identifies a problem and suggests its cause and effect, the pattern changes. The reader finds supporting details for the reasons behind an event. Another pattern is "compare and contrast" in which the author examines ideas or concepts in relationship with one another. When an author compares ideas, the reader expects to find an emphasis on their similarities; when ideas are contrasted, the focus is on their differences. Such order in writing provides a framework which the reader uses to look at ideas and add knowledge.

Exposition is one of the more widely read kinds of writing. It appears in newspapers, magazines, and in the fields of science, sports, and social sciences. Adolescents often find this type of writing stimulating because it allows them to know more about a subject in which they are interested. Since there are so many examples of this type of writing, it should be easy for the teacher or library media specialist to find sufficient materials of interest to the voracious reader as well as to the young person who is reluctant to touch a book.

Although exposition constitutes one of the largest bodies of writing, it is sometimes difficult to categorize because other forms of writing are embedded within it. Generally, exposition can be seen as magazine or newspaper articles, reports, essays, text or pamphlet material, and business letters or correspondence.

Professional Sources

The following materials may be useful as examples of types of works that are available on exposition.

An Introduction to Nonfiction, Language Arts: 5114.55. Miami, FL: Dade County Public Schools, 1972. ED 084565.

Archer, Jerome Walter, and Joseph Schwartz. *Exposition.* New York: McGraw-Hill, 1971.

Armbruster, Bonnie B., et al. "Teaching Text Structure to Improve Reading and Writing." *Reading Teacher* 43, no. 2 (November 1989), pp. 130-37.

Arena, Louis A. *Linguistics and Composition: A Method to Improve Expository Writing Skills.* Washington DC: Georgetown University Press, 1975.

Axclrod, Rise B., and Charles R. Cooper. *The St. Martin's Guide to Writing.* New York: St. Martin's Press, 1988.

Barnoske, Kathy, and Leslie Wilson. *Audience Analysis Unit for Expository Writing I.* Paper presented at the annual meeting of the Illinois Association of Teachers of English, Oak Brook, IL, October 16-18, 1980. ED 193679.

Black, Hugh C., and W. Augustus. "Expository Writing: 'Shoulds' for the 1980s." *Journal of Thought* 15, no. 2 (Summer 1980), pp. 63-68.

Christensen, Linda, et al. *A Guide to Expository Writing.* Madison, WI: University of Wisconsin Press, 1983. ED 249518.

Cox, Beverly E. "The Effects of Structural Factors on Expository Texts on Teachers' Judgments of Writing Quality." *National Reading Conference Yearbook* 39 (1990), pp. 137-43.

Curl, Mervin James. *Expository Writing.* Boston: Houghton Mifflin, 1919.

Decker, Randall E. *Patterns of Exposition.* Boston: Little, Brown, 1978.

Doll, Carol A. *Nonfiction Books for Children: Activities for Thinking, Learning, and Doing.* Englewood, CO: Teacher Ideas Press, 1990.

Englert, Carol Sue, et al. *Establishing a Case for Writing Intervention the What and Why of Expository Writing.* East Lansing, MI: Institute for Research on Teaching, Michigan State University, 1987.

Flood, James. "The Text, the Student, and the Teacher: Learning from Exposition in Middle Schools." *Reading Teacher* 39, no. 8 (April 1986), pp. 784-91.

Fulton, Maurice G. *Expository Writing: A Book of Patterns*. New York: Macmillan, 1939.

Gelman, Susan A., Sharon A. Wilcox, and Eve V. Clark. "Conceptual and Lexical Hierarchies in Young Children." *Cognitive Development* 4, no. 4 (October 1989), pp. 309-26.

Graves, Michael F., et al. "Some Characteristics of Memorable Expository Writing: Effects of Revisions by Writers with Different Backgrounds." *Research in the Teaching of English* 22, no. 3 (October 1988), pp. 242-65.

Hacker, P. M. "Language, Rules and Pseudo-Rules." *Language and Communication* 8, no. 2 (1988), pp. 159-72.

Hesse, Douglass. *Narrative in Essays: A Challenge of Textbook Truisms*. Paper presented at the annual meeting of the Conference on College Composition and Communication, Atlanta, GA, March 19-21, 1987. ED 285180.

Irmscher, William F. *Teaching Expository Writing*. New York: Holt, Rinehart and Winston, 1979.

Kar, Ronald N. *Middle School Writing: A Model Expository Paragraph Program— A Teaching Strategy*. Paper presented at the annual meeting of the National Council of Teachers of English, Chicago, IL, November 25-27, 1976. ED 143001.

Koerner, James D. *The Teaching of Expository Writing: An Exchange of Views*. New York: Alfred P. Sloan Foundation, 1977. ED 159730.

Markels, Robin Bell. *A New Perspective on Cohesion in Expository Paragraphs*. Carbondale, IL: Southern Illinois Press, 1984.

Martin, Harold Clark, and Richard M. Ohmann. *The Logic and Rhetoric of Exposition*. New York: Holt Rinehart and Winston, 1965.

Murphy, Richard. *Teaching Expository Writing. Curriculum Publication No. 16*. Berkeley, CA: Bay Area Writing Project, 1981. ED 250719.

Najimy, Norman C. *Measure for Measure: A Guidebook for Evaluating Students' Expository Writing*. Urbana, IL: National Council of Teachers of English, 1981.

Pappas, Christine C. "Young Children's Strategies in Learning the 'Book Language' of Information Books." *Discourse Processes* 14, no. 2 (April-June 1991), pp. 203-25.

Piccolo, Jo Anne. "Expository Text Structure: Teaching and Learning Strategies." *Reading Teacher* 40, no. 9 (May 1987), pp. 838-47.

Scriven, Karen. "Writing about Literature: Interpretation through Exposition." *Teaching English in the Two-Year College* 16, no. 4 (December 1989), pp. 280-83.

Unit 1003: The Language of Exposition. Minneapolis, MN: Minnesota University Press, 1968. ED 028176.

Whimby, Arthur, and Elizabeth Lynn Jenkins. *Analyze, Organize, Write: A Structured Program for Expository Writing*. Hillsdale, NJ: L. Erlbaum Associates, 1987.

Williams, Arnold. *Modern Exposition: A Textbook in Expository Writing.* New York: F. S. Crofts & Co., 1942.

Willis, Hulon. *Structure, Style, and Usage: A Guide to Expository Writing.* New York: Holt, Rinehart and Winston, 1966.

Wilson, John R. *Writing the Academic Essay.* Columbus, OH: Merrill, 1988.

The Writer's Mind: Writing as a Mode of Thinking. Urbana, IL: National Council of Teachers of English, 1983.

Zinsser, William Knowlton. *On Writing Well: An Informal Guide to Writing Non-fiction.* New York: Perennial Library, 1990.

ARTICLES

Articles, as we think of them, are usually independent sections of a larger publication. Readers find articles in encyclopedias, magazines, collected works, and newspapers. The purpose of most articles is to inform or explain an object or function, an idea, or a process. The reader expects answers to questions, such as who, what, why, when, where, and how. Therefore, the reader who comes to the text with a questioning mind is likely to be satisfied if an article on a particular topic of interest is well written.

Articles are usually set up in a manner that represents the thought process that best matches the explanation. Mirrored in many articles is a critical thinking framework or outline. Readers may encounter articles that represent sequential explanation, definition examples, compare and contrast, cause and effect, or analogy. For example, an article about volcanoes might provide a definition with examples of definitional characteristics. Also, it might provide a sequential explanation of what happens when a volcano erupts. It might even compare different eruptions that have occurred. Reading and comprehension can be improved when students learn some of the common patterns that exist in such writing. They may also gain insight by learning how to think about what questions the article is answering.

The following list contains some of the criteria that might help teachers and library media specialists judge well-written articles and collections of articles.

1. **Organization.** Is there a clear and logical progression of ideas? Did the author stick to the pattern of writing selected? Were ideas presented so that they flowed from one to the other without disruption?

2. **Accuracy.** How does the writer document the details used? What are the qualifications of the author? Are facts distinguished from opinions? Is there bias or stereotyping present in the writing?
3. **Content.** What did the writer outline as the scope of the material to be covered? Were the given details adequate to the scope? How well did the writer focus on the given subject?
4. **Style.** Did the writer present the material clearly? Was the language appropriate to the learning level or experience of the audience? What was the tone of the article? Were all these various aspects complementary to one another?

Selection of expository materials for older children is often difficult because of the wide range in the knowledge base and the interests already developed by the students. Most students like to read "nonfiction." They enjoy knowing about "real" things. Whether it is the satisfaction of learning more or confirming what they may suspect to be true, exposition is one reading option.

Professional Sources

The following list of sources are recommended as locational devices (print and automated indexes) for finding articles in periodicals. CD-ROM disks often include indexes as well as the full text of articles. Library users can expect tremendous growth and change in the use of CD-ROM material in the future.

Abridged Reader's Guide to Periodical Literature. New York: H. Wilson, 1935-. Nine Issues Yearly. Print and automated versions.

Carter, Betty, and Richard F. Abrahamson. *Nonfiction for Young Adults: From Delight to Wisdom.* Phoenix, AZ: Oryx Press, 1990.

Children's Magazine Guide: Subject Access to Children's Magazines. New Providence, NJ: R. R. Bowker, 1990-. Nine issues yearly.

Katz, Bill. *Magazines for School Libraries. Elementary, Junior High School, and High School Libraries.* New York: R. R. Bowker, 1992.

Magazine Index. Foster City, CA: Information Access. Automated and CD-ROM formats.

Magazines for Children. Glassboro, NJ: Educational Press Association of America and International Reading Association, 1990.

Magazines for Libraries. New Providence, NJ: R. R. Bowker, 1992.

Magazines for Young People: A Children's Magazine Guide Companion Volume. New Providence, NJ: R. R. Bowker, 1991.

Middle Search: A CD-ROM Reference Tool. Peabody, MA: EBSCO, 1988-. Quarterly. CD-ROM Disk.
Readers' Guide Abstracts. New York: H. W. Wilson, 1986-. Monthly, Quarterly, or Yearly. Print, microform, and automated versions.
Readers' Guide to Periodical Literature. New York: H. W. Wilson, 1900-. Print, microform, and automated versions.
Richardson, Selma K. *Magazines for Children: A Guide for Parents, Teachers, and Librarians.* Chicago: American Library Association, 1990.
Super TOM, Jr. Foster City, CA: Information Access, 1993-. Quarterly. CD-ROM Disk.

Activity: Reading for Information

The use of periodical indexes in research is not new. What is new is the extent to which the format of these indexes has changed. The activity described here is based on the use of *Time Magazine* in its electronic form. The CD-ROM *Time Almanac 1993* is a multimedia program from Compact Publishing that includes a number of menu choices for students and teachers. The "Time Weekly Issues" includes the full text of every *Time Magazine* from 1989 through January 4, 1993, an accumulation of more than 20,000 articles. "Time Highlights Decades" allows a look at what were considered the important articles and coverage in the magazine from 1923 through 1988. Under "Time Highlights Elections" students may key in on coverage of elections since 1924. A section called "Time Portraits" includes eleven in-depth articles, cover stories, and videos of personalities considered to be of major importance during the same time period. "Newsquest" lists 1,500 questions about information from 1989 to 1992. Under "United States" students can locate directories of the 103rd Congress, 400 tables from the U. S. Statistical Abstract, documents of American history, area codes, zip codes, and postal rates. Finally, under the category "World," one can find information from the *1992 CIA Worldfact Book* and *U. S. Department of State Notes* on 200 countries with color maps.

In implementing this lesson, the library media specialist should concentrate on the actual use of the program in gathering information. Students will use the menu and tool bars to access and search for information. The problem involves the ability to describe information, prioritize it, relate it to other happenings, and reorganize it into a new form.

Present the following problem to students: Pretend that you are an editor for a television or radio news program. Before beginning the new year, you want to summarize the major events of the past year. You have a deadline of 60 hours (one work week). You do not have time to read every newspaper or journal article published during the past year. You will have very little time to summarize the information. The information must fit on a single page. Choose four or five events and write short summaries based on the details you find. Your major criteria for selection of the events is the impact each event has had or will have on people and future events.

The library media specialist or classroom teacher will divide students into small heterogeneous learning groups of three or four members each. The groups should then decide how they want to function with a leader, recorder, searcher, and summarizer.

Before the students begin, the library media specialist demonstrates the use of the programs and menus, focusing on how students can make the functions on the menu serve them in solving the particular problem of their assignment. For example, browsing through the information on the CD-ROM would be interesting but not very fast. The search function is also not helpful initially, but may be later as the students consider information that should be shared. The library media specialist might suggest that students begin their search either in the "Time Highlights" menu for 1990s or the "Time Portraits." Magazine covers could also prove helpful. Students may consider the reason certain issue covers highlighted a topic.

The library specialist may discuss the method students will use to work together to scroll through the articles in the "Time Highlights." Each student may select five to ten articles he or she considers important in 1992. Then during a discussion, the students might discuss and begin to limit the events and articles, keeping the one criteria in mind. They should also rely on what they remember happened during the past year.

Each group may schedule time to practice on the machine. After practicing, the students will use the program to identify their choices for top events. When the students have identified the top five articles of their choice, they may look for the full articles describing the events. The major points of the article must be reduced to three or four sentences.

After the introduction, the library media specialist or teacher may encourage students to discuss what would constitute significance. The teacher may explain that students will be looking at newspapers as primary sources of information to find answers to this question. For this lesson, the teacher will introduce or review the pyramid for writing a newspaper article (Figure 4). This should help students skim for information and should help them understand how the authors of the articles often structure the presentation of information.

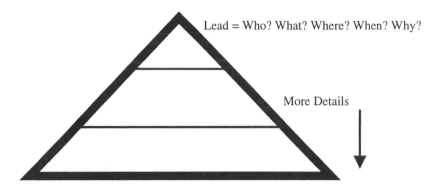

Figure 4. Pyramid for Expository Writing

The teacher may work on summarization if students show any diffi-culty in this skill. The events will be summarized and typed on one page. How does this structure help communicate information? They may also evaluate the effectiveness of using such a structure for writing articles in the newspaper and for searching later. Students may complete their searches and summaries.

The top events and articles will be shared with the other groups. Stu-dents may report on what they thought. There is likely to be disagreement on some of the selected articles or events, the groups may explain why they selected what they did and how the criteria applied. Students may discuss the use of the equipment and the problem of working under deadlines.

Activity: Reading for Main Ideas and Supporting Details

This activity allows the teacher or library media specialist to model behav-ior useful for understanding information in expository writing.

Collect and display pictures of animals, some of which are endan-gered. The pictures should be displayed so that students see them as they enter the area where the activity will take place. The library media special-ist may open a discussion about the pictures, asking what the students know about the animals depicted. Probe for comments about how many of the species still exist, where the animals are found geographically, and how the animals survive. As students offer ideas, discuss how one might find infor-mation about the animals depicted (i.e., through print and nonprint resources, and/or through direct observation of the animals, if possible).

Explain that when students use materials about animals, especially endangered species, they are using comprehension skills that involve identifying the facts and ideas that the author is trying to present. When they read information from a single source, they employ the skills necessary for identifying the main ideas and supporting details. The library media specialist will model the skills with students before sending them to look for sources independently.

Nonfiction materials that include examples of expository writing will be presented. For this exercise, Alvin, Virginia, and Robert Silverstein's *Saving Endangered Animals* from the *Better Earth Series* (1993), published by Enslow Publishers, Inc., should be selected. *Saving Endangered Animals* was chosen for this activity because of the examples of expository writing about topics related to the environment. Many of the issues presented in the book can be studied from more than one point of view. Critical reading is important for students as they form opinions and learn to understand the process by which this happens. A wide variety of materials might be selected on any chosen topic. Look for materials that include examples of topic sentences (at the beginning, in the middle, and at the end of the paragraphs). There should also be examples of paragraphs in which supporting details are provided, requiring the student to infer the main idea from these details. The material should represent various patterns of writing (e.g., compare and contrast, listing, chronology, definition by description, and cause and effect). Consult other bibliographic sources to find related materials. For example, an excellent bibliographic source of environmental books is Robert Meredith's *The Environmentalist's Bookshelf: A Guide to Best Books* (G. K. Hall, 1993).

Choose several examples from *Saving Endangered Animals* (or a similar book) to use with the students. Each example must contain a main idea with supporting ideas (details). To help students visualize the ideas, prepare overhead transparencies of selected text and overlay "frames" that highlight the main idea and supporting ideas. As each example is shown, suggest that students think about the following questions:

- What is the main idea?
- How is this idea supported?
- What are the examples or details?
- Are the details or examples appropriate?
- Do they really support the point?
- How do the examples or details support the point that the author is trying to make? [Is the author drawing comparisons and contrasts? Is

the author listing items that explain the idea? Is the author outlining a sequence of events that explain the idea (or result)? Is the author identifying the causes of an idea (or result)? Is the author listing characteristics that define an idea?]

- What words help identify relationships in the text? (For example, "if" and "then" for causal relationships, "like" or "between" for comparisons, etc.)
- How do the supporting details make the main idea seem "real"?
- Do you agree with the author's thesis, or do you have questions or opposing details and examples?

Emphasize that reading consciously to find out how the main idea is supported is one way to understand an author's point of view on controversial issues. It is also the best method of understanding the information presented in an expository text.

Some examples drawn from *Saving Endangered Animals* include:

1. Page 10 "When extinction is most likely"

   Main idea (topic sentence at beginning of paragraph): "Animals are in the greatest danger of becoming extinct when they are found in only one place or when their numbers are very small."

   Example: Heath hens
   Supporting idea: inbreeding of small heath hen population
   Supporting idea: catastrophes (fire, diseases, cats and dogs) killed heath hens

2. Page 38 "World efforts to save animals"

   Main idea (topic sentence appears in another paragraph): "Giving people an incentive to save endangered animals can be more effective than strict laws and penalties."

   Examples: Addax, African antelope
   Supporting idea: establishment of a national reserve
   Supporting idea: establishment of a sanctuary for antelope
   Supporting idea: neighboring town benefited economically from sanctuary

3. Page 13 "Society's role"

   Main idea (topic sentence at end of paragraph): "There have always been some individuals who were concerned about the fate of animals in our world."

Example: Giant sea cow
Supporting idea: Russian engineer worried about sea cow
Supporting idea: Urged authorities to ban killing
Supporting idea: Authorities did not listen

After the demonstration, have students search for interesting nonfiction materials on a particular topic. Instruct students look for three main ideas about their selected topic and give supporting details. A form for reporting the information might be helpful. Suggest to the students that understanding the concept of main ideas and supporting details will help them in the future as they take notes and develop outlines for lengthy research papers.

Sample reporting form:

Source (Author, Title, Publisher, Date, Page)

Main idea #1: _____
Supporting detail: _____
Supporting detail: _____
Supporting detail: _____
Supporting detail: _____

Main idea #2: _____
Supporting detail: _____
Supporting detail: _____
Supporting detail: _____
Supporting detail: _____

Main idea #3: _____
Supporting detail: _____
Supporting detail: _____
Supporting detail: _____
Supporting detail: _____

This activity may be followed up with a number of related activities such as the following:

- Logically arrange main ideas derived from nonfiction sources, in order to write an original paper.
- Illustrate each main idea and give supporting detail.
- Discuss the placement of topic sentences in paragraphs.
- Discuss how supporting details can justify ideas.
- Discuss why some main ideas are more difficult to support than others.

4

Persuasive Writing

INTRODUCTION

"**B**ut all the other kids get to go." Most parents have heard such statements. Usually, students learn the power of persuasion within their family structure. Most children have tried and often succeeded in persuading their parents or friends of the efficacy of some action or activity. Persuasion is a form of argumentation and involves the act of trying to convince someone of the wisdom of a certain action or thought. It draws on other forms of writing for support and is often difficult to detect unless it is standing alone.

Persuasive writing tries to establish the truth of a proposition. It proposes to convince or persuade a reader of some action or thought, and requires an emotional or attitudinal response from the reader. The author's view in this writing form should be clear. A value is expressed with the desire that the readers will adopt or change their attitudes, opinions, values, or behavior to agree with the expressed view. The study of persuasive writing suggests a study of the nature of argument, whether the pattern is logical and analytic, problem solving from content, or rhetorically generative. Such writing can either be delivered with convincing, logical arguments or can include bias, stereotypes, exceptions, overgeneralizations, and other problems that come with less thoughtful argumentation. The author "psychs out" the reader, using a strategy that appeals to the reader.

In persuasive writing, the reader confronts ideas from two or more opposing sides. Generalizations are made on all sides. Often one side is presented with supporting details, generalizations, and conclusions in such a way as to counter any arguments from the opposing side. The reader is expected to weigh pros and cons and select the author's point of view. The details may be factual and documentable, or they may have an emotional basis.

The author usually chooses words carefully and sometimes uses "loaded" words, words that he or she knows to be emotional triggers. The organizational pattern of the writing usually proceeds from simple to complex thoughts and ideas supported with details, examples, analogies, and short narratives, allowing comparisons to be made. The author uses illustrations to lead the reader to draw conclusions. Formats for persuasive writing have been formalized in editorials, informational arguments within essays, debates, political speeches and presentations, sermons, reviews, and in advertisements (Figure 5).

If a teacher or library media specialist asked students to read a sermon or a speech, the reaction would likely not be one of overwhelming joy. However, the news media is full of examples of persuasion from politicians and movie stars arguing the pros and cons of everything from what constitutes television violence to ads promoting the purchase of a specific kind of denim jeans. Students naturally give their opinions on movies and almost

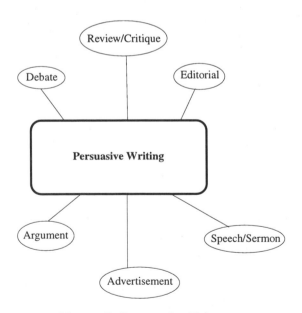

Figure 5. Persuasive Forms

every other aspect of pop culture without necessarily realizing they are engaged in the act of persuasion. Most students want to be good at the art of persuasion, because it gives them a sense of power and control over their thoughts and actions.

When these literary forms are presented in an understandable way, the motivation to read and understand is likely to be higher. A grouping of persuasive literary forms allows the teacher or library media specialist to concentrate on the higher-level critical thinking skills required to compare, contrast, evaluate, synthesize, and draw opinions. Many librarians have had the experience of trying to help a student at the reference desk find his or her own opinion on a particular issue.

Professional Sources

The following sources would be of interest to those searching for more information on persuasive writing. Subject searches for information should include terms such as *persuasive writing, persuasive discourse, persuasive rhetoric, persuasive language, persuasion,* and *argument.* More specific searches of information under the terms for types of persuasive writing (*editorial, review, criticism, speeches, addresses, sermons,* and *debate*) will also yield many valuable resources.

Anderson, Chris. *Style as Argument: Contemporary American Nonfiction.* Carbondale: Southern Illinois University Press, 1987.

Anderson, Ellen M., and Fred L. Hamel. "Teaching Argument as a Criteria-Driven Process." *English Journal* 80, no. 7 (November 1991), pp. 43-49.

Andrews, Richard, ed. *Narrative and Argument.* Philadelphia: Open University Press, 1989.

Beene, Lynn Dianne and Krystan V. Duglas. *Argument and Analysis: Reading, Thinking, Writing.* New York: Holt, Rinehart and Winston, 1989.

Beier, Ernst Gunter, and Evans G. Valens. *People-Reading: How We Control Others, How They Control Us.* New York: Stein and Day, 1975.

Black, Kathleen. "Audience Analysis and Persuasive Writing at the College Level." *Research in the Teaching of English* 23, no. 3 (October 1989), pp. 231-53.

Brand, Norman, and John O. White. *Legal Writing: The Strategy of Persuasion.* New York: St. Martin's Press, 1976.

Brashers, Howard Charles. *The Structure of Essays: Expository, Persuasive, Informal.* Englewood Cliffs, NJ: Prentice-Hall, 1972.

Brent, Doug. *Reading as Rhetorical Invention: Knowledge, Persuasion, and the Teaching of Research-Based Writing.* Urbana, IL: National Council of Teachers of English, 1992.

Cavender, Nancy, and Howard Kahane. *Argument and Persuasion: Text and Readings for Writers.* Belmont, CA: Wadsworth Publishing Co., 1989.

Crowhurst, Marion. "Interrelationships between Reading and Writing Persuasive Discourse." *Research in the Teaching of English* 25, no. 3 (October 1991), pp. 314-38.

————. "Teaching and Learning the Writing of Persuasive/Argumentative Discourse." *Canadian Journal of Education* 15, no. 4 (Fall 1990), pp. 348-59.

Cunningham, David S. *Faithful Persuasion: In Aid of a Rhetoric of Christian Theology.* South Bend, IN: University of Notre Dame Press, 1991.

Davis, Robert Edward. *Response to Innovation: A Study of Popular Argument about New Mass Media.* New York: Arno Press, 1976.

Dear, Peter. *The Literary Structure of Scientific Argument: Historical Studies.* Philadelphia: University of Pennsylvania Press, 1991.

Dinitz, Sue, and Jean Kiedaisch. "Persuasion from an Eighteen-Year-Old's Perspective: Perry and Piaget." *Journal of Teaching Writing* 9, no. 2 (Fall-Winter 1990), pp. 209-21.

Ehninger, Douglas. *Influence, Belief, and Argument: An Introduction to Responsible Persuasion.* Glenview, IL: Scott, Foresman, 1974.

Fahnestock, Jeanne, and Marie Secor. "Teaching Argument: A Theory of Types." *College Composition and Communication* 34, no. 1 (February 1983), pp. 20-30.

Fenton, Mary C. *Teaching Persuasion: A Positive Approach.* Paper presented at the annual meeting of the Wyoming Conference on Freshman and Sophomore English, Laramie, NY, June 27-July 1, 1983. ED 233396.

Govier, Trudy. *A Practical Study of Argument.* Belmont, CA: Wadsworth Publishing Co., 1985.

Graves, Harold Frank. *Argument: Deliberation and Persuasion in Modern Practice.* New York: Cordan Company, 1938.

Hinderer, Drew E. *Building Arguments.* Belmont, CA: Wadsworth Publishing Co., 1992.

Holtz, Herman. *Persuasive Writing.* New York: McGraw-Hill, 1983.

Huber, Robert B. *Influencing Through Argument.* New York: D. McKay Co., 1969.

Johannesen, Richard L. *Ethics and Persuasion: Selected Reading.* New York: Random House, 1967.

Karbach, Joan. "Using Toulmin's Model of Argumentation." *Journal of Teaching Writing* 6, no. 1 (Spring 1987), pp. 81-91.

Knudson, Ruth E. "Analysis of Argumentative Writing at Two Grade Levels." *Journal of Educational Research* 85, no. 3 (January-February 1992), pp. 169-79.

La Casce, Steward, and Terry Belanger. *The Art of Persuasion: How to Write Effectively about Almost Anything.* New York: Scribner's, 1972.

Mager, Nathan H., S. K. Mager, and P. Mager. *Power Writing, Power Speaking: 200 Ways to Make Your Words Count.* New York: Morrow, 1978.

Mayberry, Katherine J., and Robert E. Golden. *For Argument's Sake: A Guide to Writing Effective Arguments.* Glenview, IL: Scott, Foresman, 1990.

McCann, Thomas M. "Student Argumentative Writing: Knowledge and Ability at Three Grade Levels." *Research in the Teaching of English* 23, no. 1 (February 1989), pp. 62-76.

McDonald, Daniel Lamont. *The Language of Argument.* New York: Harper, 1986.

Mier, Margaret. "Strategies for Teaching Persuasive Writing." *Journal of Reading* 28, no. 2 (November 1984), pp. 172-74.

Nash, Walter. *Rhetoric: The Wit of Persuasion.* Cambridge, MA: B. Blackwell, 1989.

Newsom, Doug, and Bob Newsom. *Public Relations Writing: Form and Style.* Belmont, CA: Wadsworth Publishing Co., 1986.

Paul, Raymond, and Pellegrino W. Goione. *Perception and Persuasion: A New Approach to Effective Writing and Persuasive Speaking.* Esquire Success Videotapes, 1985. 1 videocassette. 60 min.

Ramage, John D. and John D. Bean. *Writing Arguments: A Rhetoric with Readings.* New York: Macmillan, 1992.

Rank, Hugh. *Persuasion Analysis: A Companion to Composition.* Park Forest, IL: Counter-Propaganda Press, 1988.

Roberts, R. H., and J. M. M. Good., eds. *The Recovery of Rhetoric: Persuasive Discourse and Disciplinarity in the Human Sciences.* Charlottesville, VA: University Press of Virginia, 1993.

Schell, John F. *A Heuristic for the Teaching of Persuasion.* Paper presented at the annual convention of the Modern Language Association, Los Angeles, CA, December 27-30, 1982. ED 234397.

Schmidt, Rosemarie, and Joseph F. Kess. *Television Advertising and Televangelism: Discourse Analysis of Persuasive Language.* Philadelphia: J. Benjamin's Publishing Co., 1986.

Slattery, Patrick J. "The Argumentative, Multiple-Source Paper: College Students Reading, Thinking and Writing about Divergent Points of View." *Journal of Teaching Writing* 10, no. 2 (Fall-Winter 1991), pp. 181-99.

Sproule, J. Michael. *Argument: Language and Its Influence.* New York: McGraw-Hill, 1980.

Spurgin, Sally De Witt. *The Power to Persuade: A Rhetoric and Reader for Argumentative Writing.* Englewood Cliffs, NJ: Prentice-Hall, 1985.

Stonecipher, Harry W. *Editorial and Persuasive Writing: Opinion Functions of the News Media.* New York: Hasting House, 1979.

Stygall, Gail. "Toulmin and the Ethics of Argument Fields: Teaching Writing and Argument." *Journal of Teaching Writing* 6, no. 1 (Spring 1987), pp. 93-107.

Wagner, Eileen Nause. *For the Sake of Argument: Writing Editorials and Position Papers.* Washington, DC: University Press of America, 1979.

Whately, Richard. *Elements of Rhetoric: Comprising an Analysis of the Laws of Moral Evidence and of Persuasion with Rules for Argumentative Composition and Elocution.* Carbondale, IL: Southern Illinois University Press, 1963.

Wise, William G. *The Effects of Revision Instruction on Eighth Graders' Persuasive Writing.* College Park, MD: Doctoral Dissertation, University of Maryland, 1992.

REVIEWS

Because students are often made to read a book and write about it, they may not understand the real purpose of published reviews. A review is a notice about a current book or play published in a periodical or newspaper. It is distinct from criticism, although it does include an analysis of the work. Its purposes are many. A review announces the availability of a work, describes its subject, summarizes the content, describes the author's method and the quality of the effort, compares the effort to those similar, and analyzes or evaluates all aspects of content. In other words, a review provides an opinion and strives to give the reader an accurate description of a literary or cultural event in order to persuade the reader to read or attend it. The same can be said of reviews of works in other formats.

The reader of reviews finds descriptive writing, vocabulary containing comparative words, and often logical or detailed analysis of the content structured to convince the reader that the book, movie, or tape is worth reading, viewing, or listening to.

Professional Sources

The library and education fields abound in review and selection materials. A reading of the policies of review journals would certainly be useful. The list of sources that follows will be helpful to the teacher or library media specialist searching for ideas on how to model good review writing or critiquing.

Enloe, Beverly G. "A Novel Approach to Book Reports." *Perspectives for Teachers of the Hearing Impaired* 8, no. 1 (September-October 1989), p. 6.

Kasschau, Richard A. "A Review of Book Reviews: How To Do Them Well." *Teaching of Psychology* 4, no. 1 (February 1977), pp. 41-43.

Keller, Clair W. "Using Book Reviews for Cooperative Learning." *College Teaching* 41, no. 1 (Winter 1993), pp. 26-28.

Mountain, Lee H. "The Book Reporter's TNT: Talks Need Tapes." *Journal of Reading* 19, no. 6 (March 1976), pp. 442-46.

Whittaker, Della A. "My Favorite Assignment: Reviewing Books Improves Writing Skills." *ABCA Bulletin* 43, no. 2 (June 1980), pp. 20-21.

Activity: Review Writing and Role Play

Before beginning this activity, ask students to watch the television program in which Siskel and Ebert critique current motion pictures, or another similar show that reviews books or films. Suggest that students pay attention to the methods that two people use to give their opinion about the same movie. Do they always agree? What kinds of points do the reviewers make? How do they discuss the movie to try to convince the audience that his or her particular point of view is the best? If possible, share a videotape of the program.

This particular activity has several parts. Students will have an opportunity to participate in a program in which they voice their opinions in several ways. First, ask students to contribute to creating a computerized database of book reviews, based on their own reviews of those books. Second, allow students to put their reviews on tape with the understanding that other students will be encouraged to check them out of the library media center for listening. Third, students will role play a television program in which they critique books.

The teacher and library media specialist may introduce each activity jointly or on his or her own, depending on the number of students. A database program such as *Filemaker* is recommended for setting up the file of book reviews. Creating a template to give students a format for recording their completed reviews would facilitate the learning process. At the bottom of all three activities will be the need to help students learn how to write convincing reviews.

How to Write a Thorough Book Review

Usually a well-written book review includes four parts.

Introduction to the Work. Give the bibliographic information such as author, title, publisher, and date of publication. Tell what kind of work is to be reviewed (novel, play, etc.) and what the subject of the work is. Other information about the author or format could also be given.

Sample Template

```
Author: _____

Title: _____

Publisher: _____

Date of Publication: _____

Subject: _____

Interest Level: _____

Review: _____
_____
_____
_____
_____
_____

Reviewer: _____
```

Summary. Summarize the plot or major concept of the book in one or two sentences.

Analysis. Explain the author's purpose and how the author did or did not achieve that purpose. Include a discussion of the author's style, content, tone, and method of developing the story or content. Identify strengths and weaknesses of the book.

Opinion and Recommendation. Based on the points made in the summary and analysis, explain how the book affected you and why. Explain your reaction. Conclude with your recommendation concerning whether others should read this work.

Teacher's Role

The teacher will show the students examples of reviews. One way of doing this might be to enlarge and display on an overhead projector several reviews of works that students have read. Read the review to the students, asking them to point out the major parts of a good review. As these elements are identified, discuss how each of them help the potential reader know more about the book in order to make a decision about whether or not to read it. Many indexes to periodicals and newspapers include citations of book reviews. Reviews are even available in collections. The search for reviews need not be limited to these sources, however. For example, special interest periodicals often carry book reviews. Instruct students with interests in the specific areas to locate periodicals in those specialties. In addition, most newspapers carry reviews of books, and indexes to these newspapers are helpful.

The library media specialist can stimulate students' interest by setting up a display of new books that students are not likely to have read. It would be advisable to have two copies of each title available so that two children can read the same title at the same time.When students have finished the books, have them write their own reviews. Edit and critique the first drafts of the reviews to make sure that students understand the purpose of the review. If possible, show them published reviews from review journals on the books that they have chosen. Student pairs are then ready to read the professional review as well as one another's work and to offer their evaluations of the effectiveness of both the published reviews and their own. How were their opinions similar or dissimilar to the reviews from journals and newspapers? At the conclusion of this part of the activity, students are ready to type their reviews into the database program. The value of this activity is that the database program can be made available to others who come into the library media center. If a database program is unavailable, modify the activity by supplying a notebook indexed alphabetically. Reviews of books should be typed and placed with the book titles in alphabetical order on display.

The second part of the activity is completed easily. Each pair of students who read a given title will tape record their opinion on an audiotape. Several titles on a topic and related topics or genres can be included on a given tape. Use the taped reviews to motivate other students to read the same books. After students practice taping their own voices, suggest that they add sound effects or music as background. Use audiotapes with homebound students or in a variety of other ways.

The final activity involves having students pair off and practice presenting their reviews using a television format. For a single program, select four or five titles to be reviewed. Two students read their reviews of each of the books chosen. They will need to practice together to decide on the best method for presenting their reviews. For example, one pair might decide that one will present the bibliographic information while the other summarizes the book. Both then give their analyses and opinions. After students have done this once or twice, they may be able to present their persuasive arguments in a more conversational manner. If students become very involved in the project, they may use props such as a large hand with a thumb to indicate thumbs up or thumbs down. Videotaping presentations would allow students' work to be shown to other classes. Even parents could share in the activity if videotapes were shown during parent/teacher meetings.

Presentations should be critiqued for the effectiveness of the reviews. How persuasive was each reviewer?

Student Sources

The books and indexes here are the sources most likely to be in school library media centers.

Abridged Readers' Guide to Periodical Literature. New York: H. W. Wilson, 1960.
Book Review Index. Detroit, MI: Gale Research, 1965-.
Book Review Digest. New York: H. W. Wilson, 1905-.
Children's Book Review Index. Detroit, MI: Gale Research, 1965-.
Film Review Index. Phoenix, AZ: Oryx Press, 1986-1987.
Magazine Index. Menlo Park, CA: Information Access, 1976-.
Readers' Guide to Periodical Literature. New York: H. W. Wilson, 1900-.

INFORMAL ARGUMENTS, DEBATES, AND SPEECHES

Most speeches are oral presentations. Over time, however, collections of speeches that have moved others during important historical periods have been collected into anthologies and published for the benefit of future generations or for those who were not in attendance when the speech was delivered. A speech is usually considered to be an address to an audience. This audience is most often present, but written speeches assume an audience also. Orators rely not only on the selected words, but on the delivery of those words. Written speeches rely on the power of the word itself.

For the adolescent, the speech can be powerful in that someone has a strong opinion or feeling about an issue and wants to express it. The speech is an effort to express the thought and to convince the audience of its efficacy. For young adults trying to develop their own identities and establish themselves as separate from parents and peers, a speech on a topic of interest can be highly motivating in the formation of opinion.

There are many different kinds of speeches. A course in the art of public speaking identifies the purposes of speeches as being to inform, persuade, and to entertain, among others. The focus here is on persuasion.

Professional Sources

The sources cited here deal with the theory and teaching of public speaking. The number of resources on this topic is exceptionally great. The art of public speaking is an ancient one. If other resources are needed, a search of various catalogs under *debate, forensics, public speaking, oratory, speechwriting, speeches,* and *sermons* may be useful. Terms for database searching will sometimes differ from those cited here and might also include *oral communication.* The resources in this list include those materials useful for teaching the art of public speaking or those specific to persuasive speaking.

General

Famous American Speeches: A Multimedia History, 1850 to the Present. Phoenix, AZ: Oryx Press, 1995. CD-ROM.

Manning, Beverly. *We Shall Be Heard: An Index to Speeches by American Women, 1978 to 1985.* Metuchen, NJ: Scarecrow Press, 1988.

Miller, Marion M. *Great Debates in American History.* Metuchen, NJ: Scarecrow Press, 1970.

Mitchell, Charity. *Speech Index: Fourth Edition Supplement, 1966-1980.* Metuchen, NJ: Scarecrow Press, 1982.

Speeches of the American Presidents. New York: H. W. Wilson, 1988.

Sutton, Roberta Bliss. *Speech Index.* Metuchen, NJ: Scarecrow Press, 1966.

Sutton, Roberta Bliss. *Speech Index, 1935-1955.* New Brunswick, NJ: Scarecrow Press, 1956.

Speeches and Presentations

Print

Aver, John Jeffrey, and Edward B. Jenkinson. *Essays on Teaching Speech in High School.* Bloomington, IN: Indiana University Press, 1971.

Bergman, Richard F. *A Resource Curriculum in Public Address.* Madison, WI: Wisconsin Department of Public Instruction, 1980. ED 194940.

Blankenship, Jane, and Sara Latham Stelzner. *Speech Communication Activities in the Writing Classroom.* Urbana, IL: ERIC Clearinghouse on Reading and Communication Skills, 1979.

Bock, Douglas G., and E. Hope Bock. *Evaluating Classroom Speaking.* Annandale, VA: Speech Communication Association, 1981.

Braden, Waldo W., and Mary Louise Gehring. *Speech Practices: A Resource Book for the Student of Public Speaking.* New York: Harper, 1958.

Buys, William E., Thomas Sill, and Roy Beck. *Speaking by Doing: A Speaking-Listening Text.* Lincolnwood, IL: National Textbook Co., 1987.

Cook, Jeff Scott. *The Elements of Speechwriting and Public Speaking.* New York: Collier Books, 1991.

Drazen, Joseph Gerald. *A Bibliography of Published Speeches and Concerns of Cities and Towns Found During a Search of Vital Speeches of the Day, 1958-1979.* Monticello, IL: Vance Bibliographies, 1980.

Frank, Robert L. "The Abuse of Evidence in Persuasive Speaking." *National Forensic Journal* 1, no. 2 (Fall 1983), pp. 97-107.

Gard, Grant G. *The Art of Confident Public Speaking.* Englewood Cliffs, NJ: Prentice Hall, 1986.

Hurst, Charles, and Lewis H. Fenderson. *Effective Expression: A New Approach to Better Speaking.* Columbus, OH: Merrill, 1965.

Jensen, Keith, and David C. Carter. "Self-Persuasion: The Effects of Public Speaking on Speakers." *Southern Speech Communication Journal* 46, no. 2 (Winter 1981), pp. 163-74.

Kaplan, Burton. *The Manager's Complete Guide to Speech Writing.* New York: Free Press, 1988.

Katula, Richard. "Significant Speeches from the Golden Age of American Oratory (1828-1928)." *Civic Perspective* 4, no. 3 (Fall 1991), p. 5.

Kelley, Jr., Joseph J. *Speechwriting: A Handbook for All Occasions.* New York: New American Library, 1981.

———. *Speechwriting: The Master Touch.* Harrisburg, PA: Stackpole Books, 1980.

Leeds, Dorothy. *PowerSpeak: The Complete Guide to Persuasive Public Speaking and Presenting.* New York: Prentice Hall, 1988.

Leth, Pamela C. and Steven A. Leth. *Public Communication.* Menlo Park, CA: Cummings Publishing Co., 1977.

Mager, N. H., S. K. Mager, and P. S. Mager. *Power Writing, Power Speaking: 200 Ways to Make Your Words Count*. New York: Morrow, 1978.

Marsh, Patrick O. *Persuasive Speaking: Theory, Model, Practice*. New York: Harper and Row, 1967.

McCarthy, Edward H. *Speechwriting: A Professional Step-by-Step Guide for Executives*. Dayton, OH: Executive Speaker Co., 1989.

Mohrmann, G. P. *Composition and Style in the Writing of Speeches*. Dubuque, IA: W. C. Brown Co., 1970.

Oliver, Robert Tarbell. *The Psychology of Persuasive Speech*. New York: McKay, 1963.

Oral Communication K-12 Resource Manual Version III. Baltimore, MD: Maryland State Department of Education, 1982.

Painter, Margaret. *Educator's Guide to Persuasive Speaking*. Englewood Cliffs, NJ: Prentice Hall, 1966.

Prochnow, Herbert Victor. *Speakers and Toastmasters Handbook*. Rochlin, CA: Prima Publishing and Communications, 1990.

Reid, Lynn Dudley. *Teaching Speech*. New York: McGraw-Hill, 1971.

Scheidel, Thomas Maynard. *Persuasive Speaking*. Glenview, IL: Scott Foresman, 1967.

Shoughnessy, Michael F., and Michelle Marquez. *Thirty Days and Thirty Ways Towards Better Public Speaking*. New Mexico: 1991. ED 331108.

Surles, Lynn, and W. A. Stanbury, Jr. *The Art of Persuasive Talking*. New York: McGraw-Hill, 1960.

Tarver, Jerry. *The Corporate Speech Writer's Handbook: A Guide for Professionals in Business, Agencies, and the Public Sector*. New York: Quorum Books, 1987.

Welsh, James J. *The Speech Writing Guide: Professional Techniques for Regular and Occasional Speakers*. New York: Wiley, 1978.

Nonprint

Be Prepared to Speak: A Step-by-Step Video Guide to Public Speaking. San Francisco, CA: Kantola-Skeie Productions, 1985. 27 min. 1 videocassette.

Covert, Anita. *Public Speaking*. East Lansing, MI: Michigan State University, 1978. 16 min. One 16mm film.

How to Make a Public Speech. New York: McGraw-Hill, 1986. 45 min. 1 videocassette.

How to Speak with Confidence. Chicago: Nightingale-Conant Video, 1987. 46 min. 1 videocassette.

Persuasive Speaking: Making Effective Speeches and Presentations. Esquire Success Videos, 1985. 60 min. 1 videocassette.

Periodicals

Vital Speeches of the Day. Southold, NY: City News Publishing, 1934-. Semi-monthly.

Activity: Speech

The goal of this lesson is to assist students in developing their own set of criteria for listening to speeches.

During political campaigns, television and radio news are filled with excerpts of people making speeches. Each year the president gives a state of the union address. Some speeches seem to resonate long after they are delivered, while others are considered ho-hum. Some speeches incite people toward noble goals, while others seem to do the opposite. In this activity, the library media specialist and teacher will provide students with examples of speeches to read, listen to, and watch. There are a number of examples that might be used.

Give students a chance to look at the same speech in three formats. Then have them evaluate what each format does and which format they think is most powerful. One of the more well-known examples is the speech made by Dr. Martin Luther King, Jr., "I Have a Dream," delivered on August 28, 1963. The library media specialist can help students obtain a copy of the speech, which they will read. It is available in many print sources like *A Testament of Hope: The Essential Writings of Martin Luther King, Jr.* (Harper, 1986) as well as on Internet sources. Several cassette tape versions of the speech are available. There are also films and videotapes of it. After students have read the speech, they will listen to a video or film version such as *"I Have a Dream" The Life of Martin Luther King* (CBS News, 1968), *Eyes on the Prize* (PBS Video, 1987), *Great Speeches, Volume 1*, Video, 1986), and *In Remembrance of Martin* (PBS Video, 1988).

By the time they have read, listened to, and watched the speech, students will be ready to discuss it in terms of the content and message as well as their own feelings about it. For example, what was King trying to say and what was the persuasive message? Most students will note the emotional difference between seeing and reading a speech. Some will probably identify the reading of the speech as the experience that allows them to think about the words longer.

Following this introduction to speeches, the library media specialist can provide students with lists of available audiovisual speech sources. Allow students to decide on a speech they wish to read in depth. They may want to make their selections based on the person who made the speech. Another means of finding speeches is to have students watch the newspaper for them. Some of the questions students will want to raise when reading the speeches they have selected are as follows:

- What is the important issue addressed in the speech? What is the point of the speechmaker's argument?
- What qualities make the speech a successful one? (Make a list of the good characteristics of speeches discovered from reading and observing and listening to speeches.)
- What does the speaker do to persuade his audience?
- What is appealing to you as a listener or reader?
- Would you have been or were you persuaded in the speech?
- What are the differences between being persuaded and being influenced by something, if any?

Student Sources

The sources cited can be used with many students depending on the student's age, maturity and interest level, and skill. The following materials include two types: sources of speeches and sources on giving and writing speeches. It indicates the general interest level of the material.

Print

Brandt, Carl G. *Selected American Speeches on Basic Issues, 1850-1950.* Boston: Houghton Mifflin, 1960. IL: 8-9+.

Copeland, Lewis, and Laurence Lamm. *The World's Greatest Speeches.* New York: Dover, 1958. IL: 7-9+.

Ehrlich, Henry. *Writing Effective Speeches.* New York: Paragon House, 1992. IL: 7-9+.

King, Jr., Martin Luther. *A Testament of Hope: The Essential Writings of Martin Luther King, Jr.* New York: Harper and Row, 1986. IL: 7-9+.

Meltzer, Milton. *The Black Americans: A History in Their Own Words, 1619-1983.* New York: Harper and Row/Crowell, 1984. IL: 7-9.

The President: Preacher, Teacher, Salesman: Selected Presidential Speeches, 1933-1983. Wellesley, MA: World Eagle, 1985. IL: 7-9+.

Smith, Terry C. *Making Successful Presentations: A Self-Teaching Guide.* New York: Wiley, 1991. IL: 8-9+.

Starr, Douglas P. *How to Handle Speechwriting Assignments.* New York: Pilot Books, 1978. IL: 8-9+.

Vassallo, Wanda. *Speaking with Confidence: A Guide for Public Speakers.* White Hall, VA: Betterway Pubs., 1990. IL: 8-9+.

Wrage, Ernest J. *American Forum—Speeches on Historic Issues.* New York: Harper and Row, 1960. IL: 8-9+.

Nonprint

Abraham Lincoln. New Rochelle, NY: Spoken Arts SAC 6049. 22 min. 1 audio-cassette.

Address to Congress after Pearl Harbor. Guilford, CT: J. Norton 124. 36 min. 1 audiocassette.

Address to U. S. Congress, Feb, 18, 1943. Guilford, CT: J. Norton 122. 20 min. 1 audiocassette.

Anti-Communist Voices of Yesterday (1951-1952). Guilford, CT: J. Norton 123. 44 min. 1 audiocassette.

Communicating Successfully: How to Make a More Effective Speech. Lesson I. Time Life. 25 min. One 16mm film

Great American Indian Speeches. New York: Caedmon SWC 2082. 1 audiocassette.

Great American Speeches: 1775-1896. New York: Caedmon SWC 2016. 2 audio-cassettes.

Great American Speeches: 1898-1918. New York: Caedmon 2031. 2 audiocassettes.

Great American Speeches: 1931-1947. New York: Caedmon SWC 2033. 2 audio-cassettes.

Great American Speeches: 1950-1963. New York: Caedmon SWC 2035. 2 audio-cassettes.

Great American Women's Speeches. New York: Caedmon SWC 2067. 2 audiocassettes.

Great Black Speeches. New York: Caedmon SWC 2070. 2 audiocassettes.

Great British Speeches: 1597-1625. New York: Caedmon SWC 2061. 2 audiocassettes.

Great British Speeches: 1628-1780. New York: Caedmon SWC 2062. 2 audiocassettes.

Great British Speeches: 1783-1812. New York: Caedmon SWC 2063. 2 audiocassettes.

Great British Speeches: 1867-1940. New York: Caedmon SWC 2065. 2 audiocassettes.

Great Speeches. Volume I. Alliance Video/Educational Video, 1986. 20 min. 1 videocassette.

Great Speeches. Volume II. Alliance Video/ Educational Video, 1986. 105 min. 1 videocassette.

Great Speeches. Volume III. Alliance Video/ Educational Video, 1986. 120 min. 1 videocassette.

Great Speeches. Volume IV. Alliance Video/Educational Video, 1987. 156 min. 1 videocassette.

JFK's Presidential Speeches and Statements. Boston, MA: John Fitzgerald Kennedy Library. 1 audiocassette.

John F. Kennedy: The Inauguration Speech. Beverly Hills, CA: American Educational Films, 1976. 17 min. 1 videocassette.

King, Jr., Martin Luther. *Free at Last.* Detroit, MI: Motown Record Corporation, 1968. 1 record.

King, Jr., Martin Luther. *Free at Last.* Santa Monica, CA: Children's Book and Music Center MC588, 1985. 1 audiocassette.

Liberty or Death. Brookneal, VA: Patrick Henry Memorial Foundation, 1986. 1 audiocassette.

Nixon's Nineteen Seventy-four Resignation Speech. Guilford, CT: J. Norton. 469. 15 min. 1 audiocassette.

Planning Your Speech. Centron Films, 1979. 13 min. One 16mm film

Rev. Jesse Jackson: "Our Time Has Come." New York: MCA Distributors MCA 5530, 1984. 50 min. 1 audiocassette.

Voices of History: Franklin D. Roosevelt, Harry S. Truman, Dwight D. Eisenhower. New Rochelle, NY: Spoken Arts 7049. 1 audiocassette.

Watergate Crisis: An Archive of the Speeches of President Richard M. Nixon and Gerald Ford. New Rochelle, NY: Spoken Arts MK52. 6 audiocassettes.

Internet Sample

Use of the Internet will be extremely useful for students looking for copies of presidential or historical speeches. Full text of the major speeches from the 1992 presidential campaigns of Bill Clinton, George Bush, and Andre Marrou are available through Internet: gopher bigcat.missouri.edu / reference center. Historic U. S. speeches may be captured from a number of Internet sources, such as gopher wiretap.spies.com / government docs / us speeches and addresses. The titles are listed below.

Clinton State of the Union Speech, 1993.
Clinton's Inaugural Speech, 1993.
George Bush State of the Union Speech, 1992.
George C. Wallace on Civil Rights, 4 July 1964.
Gettysburg Address.
John Adams' Inaugural Address.
Kennedy's Inaugural Speech.
Lincoln's 1st Inaugural Address.
Lincoln's 2nd Inaugural Address.
Lyndon B Johnson: We Shall Overcome, 15 March 1965.
Martin Luther King: I Have a Dream.
Nelson Mandela's Speech Upon His Release, 1993.
Patrick Henry: Give Me Liberty, 1775.

Robert C Weaver: Negro as American, 16 June 1963.
Roosevelt's Quaranteen Speech, October 1937.
Thomas Jefferson's 1st Inaugural Address.
Thomas Jefferson's 2nd Inaugural Address.
Truman's Address Before Congress, 12 March 1947.
Washington's Farewell Address.

5

Procedural Writing

INTRODUCTION

A nyone who has used a cookbook, a manual for constructing a bird house, or any "how-to" or "self-help" manual revels in a sense of accomplishment when the directions are mastered and the product is completed. Students can feel a similar sense of accomplishment whether they are learning how to play better basketball, better guitar, or how to get more attention from the opposite sex. The need for directions or instructions is greatest when the action or product is believed to be something worth accomplishing. Instructions for completing a task are often not easy to decipher, so determination is an important attribute. What characteristics are helpful to the reader's ability to comprehend procedures?

Procedural writing is defined as writing that tells someone how to do something. Usually, there is a product at the end of the act of following a prescribed set of written procedures. That product might be a specific action or an object. There is a shared valuing between the reader and writer because of the desire of a specific outcome. The motivation in the situation is the reader's wish to know the steps or the how-to's necessary for completion. Knowledge is shared between the writer of directions and the reader of them. Often the writer must assume the level of the reader's prior knowledge. These assumptions place a burden on the reader for a certain level of understanding. The author places the purpose of the written word ahead of style and self-expression.

Given the underlying purpose of procedural writing, the reader is likely to encounter language that may be ambiguous to him or her. The verbal directives in task sequences are sometimes sparse. Steps in procedures are usually either listed in sequence or written in paragraphs. Well written procedural language uses very concise prose. Well written procedures are often difficult to find, particularly in some fields where technical content can overwhelm the reader or the assumed audience has been misdiagnosed by the writer. Sometimes the reader finds comparisons that help relate a new piece of information to something already known. Sentences and paragraphs are often short and sometimes begin with the verb. Use of the second person point of view and of commands predominates. Finally, the reader can often expect to find diagrams, figures, and illustrations necessary to clarify the text. Procedural discourse requires the reader's full range of inferential skills. The taxonomies of tasks in sequence and the decision points at which the reader must check for understanding require active reading.

What motivates the reader of more difficult procedural texts? Usually the reader is curious. The purpose for the reading is very strong and focused. The reader is interested in the subject and has something specific he or she wants to accomplish. The key to motivating students to learn about procedural writing is to identify procedural texts that would interest them. Sometimes, however, students do not necessarily want anyone else to know that they are interested in a particular subject. Sensitivity to the need for privacy is an essential ingredient in involving students in this learning process.

There are many kinds of procedural writing (Figure 6). For example, students are likely to encounter recipes, experiments, directions on forms, instructional manuals, and many "how to" books. These kinds of texts are

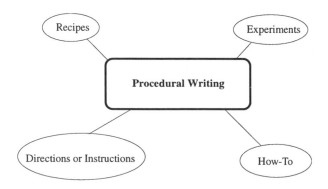

Figure 6. Procedural Forms

tered in both printed sources as well as in multimedia formats. Today, students will find books, audiotapes, videotapes, and computer databases to help them learn everything from how to apply make-up to repairing an engine. Instructions come with most of our appliances and many other purchases that require know-how to use or operate. Directions are attached to walls, displayed on signs, and seen in the media. Even so, the joke about not being able to program the VCR is not far from the truth for many of us.

Professional Sources

The study of procedural texts has continued in a number of circles. Government and business agencies are certainly eager to make sure that instructions are clear for employees and consumers. Researchers in the field of reading have looked at what children require as they learn to read. Psychologists and psycholinguists have explored the effects of structure on understanding and learning. The following articles represent a range of research and activities from all of these fields.

Allard, Lee Richard. "Analysis of Narrative and Procedural Discourse Written by Children." *Dissertation Abstracts International* 49, no. 8 (February 1989), pp. 2195A-2196A.

Ballmer, Thomas T. "Frames and Context Structures: A Study of Procedural Context Semantics with Linguistic Applications in Sentences and Textlinguistics," in *Zum Thema Sprache und Logik: Ergebnisse einer Interdisziplinaren Diskussion,* eds. Thomas Ballmer and Walter Kindt. Hamburg: Buske, 1980.

Bieger, George R., and Marvin D. Glock "Comprehending Spatial and Contextual Information in Picture-Text Instructions." *Journal of Experimental Education* 54, no. 4 (Summer 1986), pp. 181-88.

Burnham, Catherine. *Improving Written Instructions for Procedural Tasks. Working Papers.* Berkeley, CA: National Center for Research in Vocational Education, 1992. ED 351524.

Burnham, Catherine, and Thomas H. Anderson. *Learning to Sew on a Button by Reading a Procedural Text. Technical Report No. 543.* Champaign, IL: University of Illinois Press, 1991.

Coggin, William. "A Hands-On Project for Teaching Instructions." *Technical Writing Teacher* 8, no. 1 (Fall 1980), pp. 7-9.

Dixon, Peter. "Actions and Procedural Directions: Outcome of Symposium, Eugene, OR, June 1984," in *Coherence and Grounding in Discourse,* ed. Russell S. Tomlin. Amsterdam: Benjamins, 1987.

Donin, Janet, et al. "Students' Strategies for Writing Instructions: Organizing Conceptual Information in Text." *Written Communication* 9, no. 2 (April 1992), pp. 209-36.

Flavell, John H., et al. "The Road Not Taken: Understanding the Implications of Initial Uncertainty in Evaluating Spatial Directions." *Developmental Psychology* 21, no. 2 (March 1985), pp. 207-16.

Hoskins, Suzanne. "Discourse Structure Analysis: An Introduction to Procedures and Implications for Instruction." *Reading World* 24, no. 4 (May 1985), pp. 30-40.

Kieras, David E. *The Role of Prior Knowledge in Operating Equipment from Written Instructions. Final Report.* Ann Arbor, MI: Michigan University Press, 1985.

Kieras, David E., and Susan Bovair. "The Acquisition of Procedures from Text: A Production-System Analysis of Transfer of Training." *Journal of Memory and Language* 25, no. 5 (October 1986), pp. 507-24.

Kroll, Barry M. "Explaining How To Play a Game: The Development of Informative Writing Skills." *Written Communication* 3, no. 2 (April 1986), pp. 195-218.

McConkie, George W. *A Framework for Research on the Comprehension of Procedural Texts and Pictures.* Paper presented at the annual meeting of the International Reading Association, Chicago, April 26-30, 1982. ED 225100.

Milburn, Val. *Understanding Instruction.* England: Leeds City Council Department of Education, 1986. ED 279869.

Mulcahy, Patricia. "Writing Reader-Based Instructions: Strategies to Build Coherence." *Technical Writing Teacher* 15, no. 3 (Fall 1988), pp. 234-43.

Robinson, Peter J. "Procedural Vocabulary and Language Learning." *Journal of Pragmatics: An Interdisciplinary Bimonthly of Language Studies* 13, no. 4 (August 1989), pp. 523-46.

Roderman, Winifred Ho. *Reading and Following Directions.* Hayward, CA: Janus, 1978.

Schorr, Frances. *Comprehending Procedural Instructions: The Influence of Metacognitive Strategies.* Paper presented at the annual meeting of the American Educational Research Association, New York, March 19-23, 1982. ED 214130.

Schorr, Frances. *The Effects of Varying Procedural Instructions on Comprehension.* Paper presented at the annual meeting of the American Educational Research Association, New Orleans, LA, April 23-27, 1984. ED 243078.

Southland, Sherry. "Bibliography on the Writing of Instructions, Excluding Sources on Computer Documentation." *Technical Communication* 35, no. 2 (May 1988), pp. 101-104.

———. "Special Section: Usable Instructions Based on Research Theory: Part I: Introduction." *Technical Communication* 35, no. 2 (May 1988), pp. 89-90.

Starkey, Carolyn Morton. *What You Need To Know About Reading Labels, Directions, and Newspapers.* Lincolnwood, IL: National Textbook Co., 1985.

Stone, David Edey. *Test of Picture-Text Amalgams in Procedural Texts.* Paper based on doctoral dissertation. New York: Cornell University, 1977. ED 236665.

Wikberg, Kay. "Topic, Theme, and Hierarchical Structure in Procedural Discourse," in *Theory and Practice in Corpus Linguistics*, eds. Jan Aarts and William Meigs. Amsterdam: Rodopi, 1990.

EXPERIMENTS

When individuals test or demonstrate what they might consider known truths, check the validity of their hypotheses, or determine the nature of something not yet known to them, they usually engage in some kind of experimentation. Such experimentation ranges in the level of formality and criteria used to judge its success. Our daily lives include many experiments. However, written experiments are written in a definite manner and usually contain identifiable markers. The organization or structure usually includes a hypothesis, background information or rationales for the hypothesis, lists of materials or resources necessary to test the hypothesis, a procedure or outline for testing the hypothesis, and the results, often with inferences and conclusions drawn from them. When the reader encounters this structure, he or she knows that this is an experiment or study.

There are other clues or textual characteristics. The experiment requires sequential or logical thinking. The pattern of establishing a problem and then testing it requires the reader to follow a logical sequence of steps. These steps are often written in second person. Well-written text usually incorporates active rather than passive voice. Most experiments include vocabulary related to simple and complex measurement. The reader must understand these measurements and the variables involved in order to comprehend and compare them. The sequentially structured information relates to other pieces of information. Such relationships must be understood. Reading experiments often involves precise wording that makes a difference to understanding the meaning of the results.

Can such reading be boring? Yes, but it can also be stimulating to the inquiring mind, especially if the experiments relate to questions in which the reader is interested. Presenting students with options for exploring and understanding the subjects that they question can be highly motivating. Sometimes such explorations lead students to careers in the subject area. Sharing information in such forms provides students with the sense that this type of reading is both valuable and intellectually satisfying in its own right.

Professional Sources

Reference Books

Annotated List of Laboratory Experiments in Chemistry from the Journal of Chemical Education 1957-1984. ACS Education Division, Office of College Chemistry, 1986.

Bombaugh, Ruth. *Science Fair Success*. New York: Enslow, 1990.

Pilger, Mary Anne. *Science Experiments Index for Young People*. Littleton, CO: Libraries Unlimited, 1988.

———. *Science Experiments Index for Young People Update 91*. Littleton, CO: Libraries Unlimited, 1992.

Science Fairs and Projects. Washington DC: National Science Teachers Association, 1984.

Science Fairs and Projects, 7-12. Washington DC: National Science Teachers Association, 1985.

Science Fair Project Index, 1973-1980. Metuchen, NJ: Scarecrow Press, 1983.

Science Fair Project Index, 1981-1984. Metuchen, NJ: Scarecrow Press, 1986.

Science Fair Project Index, 1985-1989. Metuchen, NJ: Scarecrow Press, 1993.

Van Deman, Barry A., and Ed McDonald. *Nuts and Bolts: A Matter of Fact Guide to Science Fair Projects*. Harwood Heights, IL: Science Man Press, 1980.

Wolfe, Connie. *Search: A Research Guide for Science Fairs and Independent Study*. Tucson, AZ: Zephyr Press, 1987.

Yoshika, Ruby. *Thousands of Science Projects: Classified Titles of Exhibits Shown at Science Fairs and/or Produced as Projects for the Westinghouse Science Talent Search*. Science Service, 1987.

Reading and Writing Experiments

American Association of Physics Teachers. *Physics Demonstration Experiments*. New York: Ronald Press, 1970.

Anderson, O. Roger. *The Experience of Science: A New Perspective for Laboratory Teaching*. New York: Teachers College Press, 1976.

Bostian, Lloyd R. "How Active, Passive and Nominal Styles Affect Readability of Science Writing." *Journalism Quarterly* 60, no. 4 (Winter 1983), pp. 635-40, 670.

Bowes, John E., and Keith R. Stamm. *Science Writing Techniques and Methods: What the Research Tells Us*. Paper pesented at the annual aeeting of the Association for Education in Journalism, Seattle, Washington, August 13-16, 1978. ED 166702.

Brandt, W. W. "Practice in Critical Reading as a Method to Improve Scientific Writing." *Science Education* 55, no. 4 (October-December 1971), pp. 451-55.

Cannon, Robert E. "Experiments with Writing to Teach Microbiology." *American Biology Teacher* 52, no. 3 (March 1990), pp. 156-58.

Carr, Joseph J. *The Art of Science: A Practical Guide to Experiments, Observations, and Handling Data.* San Diego, CA: HighText Publications, 1992.

Cochener, David, and Debbie Cochener. "How Many Miles Per Hour Is That Fan Going? An Experiment to Implement Problem Solving in Grades 5-8." *School Science and Mathematics* 93, no. 3 (March 1993), pp. 158-59.

Conant, James Bryant. *The Growth of the Experimental Sciences: An Experiment in General Education Progress Reports on the Use of Case Method in Teaching the Principles of the Tactics and Strategy of Science.* Cambridge, MA: Harvard University Press, 1949.

Crothers, J. H., and A. M. Lucas. "Putting Biology Students Out to Grass: The Nettlecombe Experiment After Thirteen Years." *Journal of Biological Education* 16, no. 2 (Summer 1982), pp. 108-114.

Day, Robert A. *How to Write and Publish a Scientific Paper.* Phoenix, AZ: Oryx Press, 1988.

Eagan, Ruth. "Teaching Organization and Presentation of Reports, Involving Students as Active Participants." *Reading Improvement* 16, no. 1 (Spring 1979), pp. 62-65.

Ellman, Neil. "Science in the English Classroom: Teaching Ideas." *English Journal* 67, no. 4 (April 78), pp. 63-65.

Farmer, Mike. *Writing Science Project Research Papers: A Step-by-Step Approach.* Tigerville, SC: Applied Educational Technology, 1992. ED 356957.

Forcheri, Paola, and Maria Teresa Molfino. "The Design and Evaluation of Teaching Experiments in Computer Science." *Educational and Training Technology International* 29, no. 2 (May 1992), pp. 94-104.

Giese, Ronald N., et al. "Teaching Experiment Design to Beginning and Advanced Students: Procedure Writing—But This Ain't No English Class." *Science Activities* 26, no. 1 (February-March 1989), pp. 24-27.

Goodman, W. Daniel, and John C. Bean. "A Chemistry Laboratory Project To Develop Thinking and Writing Skills." *Journal of Chemical Education* 60, no. 6 (June 1983), pp. 483-85.

Gratz, Ronald K. "Improving Lab Report Quality by Model Analysis, Peer Review, and Revision." *Journal of College Science Teaching* 19, no. 5 (March-April 1990), pp. 292-95.

Greene, Paul F. "Preparation of Scientific Papers." *American Biology Teacher* 51, no. 7 (October 1989), pp. 438-39.

Gubanich, Alan A. "Writing the Scientific Paper in the Investigative Lab." *American Biology Teacher* 39, no. 1 (January 1977), pp. 27-34.

Hegarty-Hazel, Elizabeth. *The Student Laboratory and the Science Curriculum.* New York: Routledge, 1990.

Jacobson, Cliff. *Water, Water Everywhere, But . . . . Notes for the Teacher, Report Writing Directions and Experiments.* Loveland, CO: Hach Company, 1983. ED 231654.

Lang, Thomas A. "A Technical Writing Laboratory: The Puzzle Exercise." *Technical Writing Teacher* 15, no. 2 (Spring 1988), pp. 132-37.

Kanare, Howard M. *Writing the Laboratory Notebook.* Washington, DC: American Chemical Society, 1985. ED 344734.

Mayer, Bernadette. "Science Writing Experiments." *Teachers and Writers Magazine* 19, no. 5 (May-June 1988), pp. 6-10.

Monroe, Judson, et al. *The Science of Scientific Writing.* Dubuque, IA: Kendall/Hunt Publishing Company, 1977. ED 133743.

Nasca, Donald. *Effect of Varied Presentations of Laboratory Exercises Within Programmed Materials on Specific Intellectual Factors of Science Problem Solving Behavior.* Brockport, NY: State University College at Brockport, 1965.

Paulu, Nancy. *Helping Your Child Learn Science.* Washington, DC: U. S. Department of Education, 1991.

Pechenik, Jan A., and Jay Shiro Tashiro. "Instant Animals & Conceptual Loops. Teaching Experimental Design, Data Analysis & Scientific Writing." *American Biology Teacher* 53, no. 4 (April 1991), pp. 220-28.

Reflections on Writing in Science. Scientific Insight. Laboratory Report. Albany, NY: Bureau of General Education Curriculum Development, New York State Education Department, 1981. ED 222336.

Ross, Frederick C., and Mitchell H. Jarosz. "Integrating Science Writing: A Biology Instructor and an English Teacher Get Together." *English Journal* 67, no. 4 (April 1978), pp. 51-55.

Ross, John A., and Florence J. Maynes. "Experimental Problem Solving: An Instructional Improvement Field Experiment." *Journal of Research in Science Teaching* 20, no. 6 (September 1983), pp. 543-56.

Rossi, Jean Pierre. "The Function of Frame in the Comprehension of Scientific Text." *Journal of Educational Psychology* 82, no. 4 (December 1990), pp. 727-32.

Sanford, James F. *Multiple Drafts of Experimental Laboratory Reports.* Paper presented at the annual meeting of the American Psychological Association, Washington, DC, August 23-27, 1982. ED 226375.

Sawyer, Thomas M. *The Organization of Reports of Scientific Experiments.* Paper presented at the annual meeting of the Conference on College Composition and Communication, San Francisco, CA, March 18-20, 1982. ED 214190.

Schlenker, Richard M. *A Guide to Writing Student Laboratory and Field Research Reports.* 1978. ED 160437.

Schlenker, Richard M., and Constance M. Perry. *A Writing Guide for Student Oceanography Laboratory and Field Research Reports.* 1979. ED 178332.

Scouten, Edward L. "The Laboratory Report: An Instructional Module for Technical English." *American Annals of the Deaf* 124, no. 3 (June 1979), pp. 377-80.

Sheldon, Daniel S., and John E. Penick. *Favorite Labs from Outstanding Teachers. Monograph VII.* Reston, VA: National Association of Biology Teachers, 1991. ED 359063.

Solomon, Joan. *Teaching Children in the Laboratory.* London: Croom Helm, 1980.

Totten, Samuel, and Claire Tinnin. "Incorporating Writing into the Science Curriculum: A Sample Activity." *Science Activities* 25, no. 4 (November-December 1988), pp. 25-29.

United Nations Educational, Scientific and Cultural Organization. *700 Science Experiments for Everyone: Originally Published as UNESCO Sourcebook for Science Teaching.* Garden City, NY: Doubleday, 1958.

Van Cleave, Janice Pratt. *Teaching the Fun of Physics: 101 Activities to Make Science Education Easy and Enjoyable.* Englewood Cliffs, NJ: Prentice-Hall, 1985.

Vargas, Marjorie Fink. "Writing Skills for Science Labs." *Science Teacher* 53, no. 8 (November 1986), pp. 29-33.

Walker, J. R. L. "A Student's Guide to Practical Write-Ups." *Biochemical Education* 19, no. 1 (January 1991), pp. 31-32.

Wilkes, John. "Science Writing: Who? What? How?" *English Journal* 67, no. 4 (April 1978), pp. 56-60.

Worsley, Dale, and Bernadette Mayer. *The Art of Science Writing.* New York: Teachers & Writers Collaborative, 1989.

Wyatt, H. V. "Writing, Tables, and Graphs: Experience with Group Discussions in Microbiology Practical Work." *Journal of Biological Education* 18, no. 3 (Fall 1984), pp. 239-45.

Activity: Laboratory Experimentation

Locate a suitable place either in the library media center or in the classroom laboratory for experimenting. References and books including experiments should be collected and a long list of available books on experiments should be arranged by subject and duplicated for distribution. The books and bibliographies need to be available during the first session with students. The books of experiments should be grouped by subject area. Samples of the equipment or tools that might be encountered in the experiments should be displayed if possible.

At the first session, explain that students will have an opportunity to think about subjects that will be interesting to explore. The bibliographies will be used by students while they explore the materials freely. The students will "browse before buying." Explain further that the students will read certain forms of writing because the information in the sources explores some experimental aspect of the subject. The students will browse or skim references that have been provided to observe the arrangement of the information and note the help that the materials give the reader. Allow the students time to explore and read. Suggest ways to browse and read, such as:

- reading the title page and table of contents
- reading the jacket blurbs of the books
- skimming the chapter headings and subheadings
- selecting a particular chapter to see how the material is organized
- identifying the kinds of information that are presented in a selected chapter.

After the students have finished browsing, they may gather to discuss the elements that they noted while they were browsing. What elements were included in the books? Discuss these elements with students:

- problem or question (background on problem)
- hypothesis (purpose or rephrasing of question)
- outline of strategy for exploring the problem (methodology)
- resources needed
- outline of procedures
- data collected
- conclusion and discussion

As the students discuss the elements, they may comment on the books or sources that were most appealing. Books containing experiments are not always meant to be read straight through. It is completely legitimate to jump around from chapter to chapter or section to section. In other words, the purpose for reading books of experiments is different from the purpose for reading other types of books.

Following the discussion, the students might focus on one particular interest area and read as many experiments as possible on that subject. Introduce students to indexes of experiments. Suggest that they try at least two or three of the experiments. Based on their own experimentation, they will get some ideas for other experiments that might be performed. They will develop and write their own experiment for other classmates to try. The student-prepared experiments can be entered into a computer database to be accessed by others. Students may find classmates who are interested in the same topics they are. Students must try to convince their classmates to try the experiments.

Student Sources

The following books are representative of the many books indexed in the reference section on experiments. Encourage students to read the works if only for the intellectual stimulation provided. As before, IL indicates general interest level.

Barr, George. *Outdoor Science Projects for Young People.* New York: Dover, 1991. IL: 5-8.

Carr, Joseph J. *The Art of Science: A Practical Guide to Experiments, Observations, and Handling Data.* San Diego, CA: HighText Publications, 1992. IL: 7-9+.

Challand, Helen J. *Activities in Physical Sciences.* Chicago: Children's Press, 1984. IL: 4-7.

————. *Science Projects and Activities.* Chicago: Children's Press, 1985. IL: 4-7.

Cobb, Vicki. *Chemically Active! Experiments You Can Do at Home.* Philadelphia: Lippincott, 1985. IL: 6-9.

————. *The Secret Life of Hardware: A Science Experiment Book.* Philadelphia: Lippincott, 1982. IL: 5-8.

Ehrlich, Robert. *Turning the World Inside Out and 174 Other Simple Physics Demonstrations.* Princeton, NJ: Princeton University Press, 1990. IL: 8-9+.

Gardner, Robert. *Energy Projects for Young Scientists.* New York: Watts, 1989. IL: 5-8.

————. *More Ideas for Science Projects.* New York: Watts, 1989. IL: 7-9.

Goodwin, Peter H. *Engineering Projects for Young Scientists.* New York: Watts, 1989. IL: 5-8.

————. *Physics Projects for Young Scientists.* New York: Watts, 1991. IL: 7-9.

Herbert, Don. *Mr. Wizard's Experiments for Young Scientists.* New York: Doubleday, 1990. IL: 5-8.

Historical Science Experiments on File: Experiments, Demonstrations, and Projects for the School and Home. New York: Facts on File, 1993. IL: 5-9+.

Iritz, Maxine Haren. *Blue Ribbon Science Fair Projects.* Blue Ridge Summit, PA: Tab Books, 1991. IL: 7-9.

Learning About What Scientists Do. Chicago: SVE, 1984. 4 sound filmstrips.

Liem, Tik L. *Invitations to Science Inquiry.* Lexington, MA: Ginn, 1981.

McKay, David W., and Bruce G. Smith. *Space Science Projects for Young Scientists.* New York: Watts, 1986. IL: 6-9.

Millspaugh, Ben. *Aviation and Space Science Projects.* Blue Ridge Summit, PA: Tab Books, 1991. IL: 7-9.

More Science Experiments on File: Experiments, Demonstrations, and Projects for School and Home. New York: Facts on File, 1990. IL: 5-9+.

Munson, Howard R. *Science Experiences with Everyday Things.* David S. Lake Publisher, 1988. IL: 5-9+.

Nature Projects on File. New York: Facts on File, 1992. IL: 5-9+.

Newton, David E. *Science/Technology/Society Projects for Young Scientists.* New York: Watts, 1991. IL: 5-8.

Parker, Steve. *The Marshall Cavendish Library of Science Projects.* New York: Marshall Cavendish, 1989. IL: 5-8.

Rainis, Kenneth G. *Nature Projects for Young Scientists.* New York: Watts, 1989. IL: 5-8.

Science Experiments on File: Experiments, Demonstrations, and Projects for School and Home. New York: Facts on File, 1988. IL: 5-9+.

Science in Action: The Marshall Cavendish Guide to Projects and Experiments. New York: Marshall Cavendish, 1988. IL 7-9+.

Tocci, Salvatore. *Biology Projects for Young Scientists.* New York: Watts, 1989. IL: 5-8.

———. *How To Do a Science Fair Project.* New York: Watts, 1986. IL: 5-8.

Van Cleave, Janice. *Janice Van Cleave's Molecules.* New York: John Wiley, 1992. IL: 5-8.

RECIPES

A clue to something delicious? A recipe is a written set of procedures through which individuals read and follow planned, carefully presented examples of behavior that will lead to some desired product or result. The procedures incorporate the use of certain techniques, materials, equipment, and steps that are prescribed to obtain a specific outcome. Cooks who are good at reading recipes and have some knowledge of the vocabulary can often tell how a particular recipe will turn out. For the less able cook, recipes are often the only thread connecting them to palatable sustenance.

Eating is one of the basics in survival, and students usually enjoy experimenting with ingredients to create some dish of their own. The benefits of stirring, kneading, sifting, cutting, dicing, and so forth can be seen in the immediate eating of the final product. Efforts can also be quickly evaluated. Students can easily see the results of their ability to follow a set of instructions.

Recipes usually include a description of the product. This description can be a title, a phrase, or a paragraph. The description is almost always followed by a list of ingredients. This list will include the foodstuffs necessary and, in more basic lists, the equipment that will be used. Either in a list or sequential paragraph or set of paragraphs, the steps required to complete the recipe follow. Some recipes assume that the reader knows basic terminology, while others describe all actions necessary to complete the task.

Students are usually highly motivated about cooking. It is fun to follow a set of steps correctly and finish with a very usable product, especially if it tastes good.

Professional Sources

The following reference sources are useful for finding recipes or cookbooks in specific areas. The articles and books on teaching methods will be useful to some.

Reference Books

Axford, Lavonne B. *English Language Cookbooks, 1600-1973*. Detroit: Gale Research Company, 1976.

Brown, Eleanor Parker, and Bob Brown. *Culinary Americana; Cookbooks Published in the Cities and Towns of the United States of America During the Years from 1860 through 1960*. New York: Roving Eye Press, 1961.

Cookbooks and Good Eating Cookbooks for Special Populations: Let's Eat. Lansing, MI: PAM Assistance Centre, 1990.

Cook's Choice: A Selection of Recipes from Rare and Important Cookbooks from the Ninth to the Nineteenth Century. Philadelphia: Rosenbach Museum & Library, 1982.

National Diabetes Information Clearinghouse. *Cookbooks for People with Diabetes: Selected Annotations*. Bethesda, MD: U. S. Department of Health and Human Services, 1981.

National Diabetes Information Clearinghouse. *Supplement to Cookbooks for People with Diabetes*. Bethesda, MD: U. S. Department of Health and Human Services, 1984.

Shih, Tian-Chu. *Health Related Cookbooks: A Bibliography*. Metuchen, NJ: Scarecrow Press, 1991.

Teaching Method

Axler, Bruce H. *Methods and Manners of Cooking: The Fundamentals of Cooking Presented as an Aid to People Who Learn to Cook by Cooking*. New York: Funk & Wagnalls, 1969.

Barchers, Suzanne I., and Patricia C. Marden. *Cookin' Up U. S. History: Recipes and Research to Share With Children*. Littleton, CO: Libraries Unlimited, 1991.

Brown, Virginia. "On Reviewing Cookbooks: From Kitchen to Classroom." *Journal of Learning Disabilities* 9, no. 2 (February 1976), pp. 63-68.

Dirks, Moses, and Lydia Dirks. *Niigugim Qalgadangis (Atkan Food)*. Anchorage, AK: University of Alaska Press, 1978. ED 173042.

Eshelman, Martha. "Read to Eat: A Teaching Strategy." *Instructor* 97, no. 8 (April 1988), pp. 34-36.

Fisher, Julie. "What's in the Pot?" *Mathematics Teacher* 86, no. 3 (March 1993), pp. 214-15.

Goldstein, Bobbye S. "What's Cooking in the Reading Program?" *Reading Teacher* 28, no. 1 (October 1974), pp. 22-25.

Hopkins, Lee Bennett. "Here, Taste This: Cooking with Children's Literature." *Teacher* 96, no. 3 (November 1978), pp. 22, 24, 26.

Lewis, Gail, and Jean M. Shaw. *Recipes for Learning: Exploring the Curriculum through Cooking.* Santa Monica, CA: Goodyear Publishing Company, 1979.

McAfee, Oralie, Evelyn W. Haines, and Barbara Bullman Young. *Cooking and Eating with Children: A Way to Learn.* Washington, DC: Association for Childhood Education International, 1974.

Mix, Stir, Blend: A Pantry of Cooking Activities and Ideas for Elementary K-6. Oklahoma City, OK: Oklahoma State Department of Education, 1982.

Morrow, Lesley M. "Stories Good Enough to Eat." *Instructor* 93, no. 1 (August 1983), pp. 22-23, 25.

Multicultural Cooking with Kids. Chicago: Lakeshore Learning Materials, 1991.

Norton, Kent. "Teaching Cooking as an Alternative to Force-Feeding Facts." *Journal for the Education of the Gifted* 2, no. 2 (Winter 1979), pp. 106-14.

Renoudet, Virginia V. *Recipes for Kids.* Washington, DC: Department of the Air Force, 1989.

Routledge, Joan. "What's Cooking?" *Arithmetic Teacher* 33, no. 2 (October 1985), pp. 14-15.

Smith, Rosalind Bingham. "Teaching Mathematics to Children Through Cooking." *Arithmetic Teacher* 21, no. 6 (October 1974), pp. 480-84.

Waxter, Julia B. *The Science Cookbook: Experiment-Recipes that Teach Science and Nutrition.* Belmont, CA: Fearon Teacher Aids, 1981.

Activity: Demonstration

Prior to this activity, encourage students to view several cooking shows on television. For those without access to such programs, obtain several videotapes for showing in the classroom. Suggest that students watch actions that take place in the videotapes, personalities on the shows, the tone, and the purpose of the shows.

On the day of the introduction to the activity, set up a very simple cooking demonstration. For more drama, come in a costume or with props and decide on a special theme. Themes relating to holidays or even something as silly as a "Where's Elvis?" motif (food that Elvis might have liked) are appropriate and fun. Another focus might be on the food itself, such as the *solanum tuberosum,* the potato, a new world food. One idea might be to use displays of potatoes dressed like Mr. Potatohead, from the old game, to introduce simple recipes for French fries, mashed potatoes, stuffed potatoes, etc. The emphasis then becomes following a sequence of directions. The text of the selected recipe should be enlarged so that students either have copies or have visual access to the ingredients and necessary steps. Use an overhead projector or chart.

In this case, the demonstration should follow a very simple format.

1. Present a peppy introduction. Samples of what will be cooked may already be prepared and displayed.
2. State the purpose of the demonstration clearly and precisely. The students should know what recipe is being tried and how to tell if the effort is a success.
3. Have all equipment prominently displayed so that the materials necessary for the task are obvious. Make sure that students understand that the equipment should be set up and ready to go before the process begins.

During demonstrations, stick to the scripted steps. Specific instructions should be short and concise. The language used to describe should be essential to the demonstration. Often the demonstrator will give commands. Make sure that each command is in the proper sequence. All the observers should be able to see each step of the demonstration. If this is a problem, tables with mirrors suspended over them are often used. A video camera with television screen would also enable everyone to observe at close range.

Most demonstrators state the step, demonstrate it, and then repeat the step. The idea is to reinforce each step in the sequence. Sometimes it is helpful to have examples of what can happen if a particular step is done incorrectly. For example, if the cooking of the food is not timed correctly, the food may either be burned or undercooked. A few examples may be helpful if the procedure is especially tricky or unfamiliar to the audience. When the food is ready, everyone can share it.

Usually following a demonstration, the students or audience have a practice session with the leader, providing guided practice opportunities. In this case, the students will be able to practice later in the lesson. Their activity and follow-up are to pick a theme and plan one meal around the theme. The food selected must be nutritious, appetizing, and within a given budget. Part of the assignment is for students to find the recipes they will use, calculate the cost of the ingredients, and prepare the recipes as a demonstration to the rest of the class. The theme of the students' demonstration may be serious or humorous. This activity, if successful, could become the impetus for an afternoon cooking club for students interested in food and the culinary arts. Local chefs, cooks, or home arts people could be invited routinely to work with students who want to participate.

Student Sources

Cookbooks abound! There are now cookbooks for almost all ethnic groups, holidays, specific types of cooking equipment, diets, specific foods, and budgets. The following works are representative of these variations in cookbooks. Interest levels have been noted, although recipes may be appropriate for a wide range of ages. Alert students to the sections of the newspaper and to magazines where new recipes are printed.

The following list includes several classic cookbooks and a sampling of newer titles that will appeal to students in grades five through nine.

Aeschliman, Bonnie. *Step by Step Microwave Cooking for Boys and Girls.* Nashville, TN: Ideals Publishing Corporation, 1985. IL: 5-8.

Albyn, Carole Lisa, and Lois Sinaiko Webb. *The Multicultural Cookbook for Students.* Phoenix, AZ: Oryx Press, 1993. IL: 5-8+.

Amari, Suad. *Cooking the Lebanonese Way.* Minneapolis, MN: Lerner Publications, 1985. IL: 4-7.

Anderson, Gretchen. *The Louisa May Alcott Cookbook.* Boston: Little, Brown, 1985. IL: 4-7. RL: 7.

Anderson, Jean, and Hanna Elaine. *The New Doubleday Cookbook.* New York: Doubleday, 1985. IL: 7-9+.

Andreev, Tania. *Food in Russia.* Vero Beach, FL: Rourke Publications, 1989. IL: 6-9.

Bacon, Josephine. *Cooking the Israeli Way.* Minneapolis, MN: Lerner Publications, 1986. IL: 6-9. RL: 7.

Better Homes and Gardens After-school Cooking. Des Moines, IA: Meredith Corp., 1987. IL: 4-7.

Better Homes and Gardens Cookies for Kids. Des Moines, IA: Meredith Corp., 1983. IL: 4-7; RL: 7.

Better Homes and Gardens Microwave Cooking for Kids. Des Moines, IA: Meredith Corp., 1984. IL: 4-7.

Bisignano, Alphonse. *Cooking the Italian Way.* Minneapolis, MN: Lerner Publications, 1982. IL: 6-9.

Blain, Diane. *The Boxcar Children Cookbook.* Morton Grove, IL: A. Whitman, 1991. IL: 4-7.

Blanchard, Marjorie Page. *The Outdoor Cookbook.* New York: Watts, 1977. IL: 5-8.

Cadwallader, Sharon. *Cooking Adventures for Kids.* Boston: Houghton Mifflin, 1974. IL: 4-7.

Christian, Rebecca. *Cooking the Spanish Way.* Minneapolis, MN: Lerner Publications, 1982. IL: 6-9.

A Christmas Sampler of Feasts: With Recipes from Various Cookbooks. Garden City, NY: Doubleday, 1981. IL: 7-9+.

Chung, Okwha, and Judy Monroe. *Cooking the Korean Way.* Minneapolis, MN: Lerner Publications, 1988. IL: 6-9.

Coronado, Rosa. *Cooking the Mexican Way.* Minneapolis, MN: Lerner Publications, 1982. IL: 6-9.

Cox, Beverly, and Martin Jacobs. *Spirit of the Harvest: North American Indian Cooking.* New York: Stewart, Tabor & Chang, 1991. IL: 6-9+

Crocker, Betty. *Betty Crocker's Best Recipes of the Year.* New York: Prentice-Hall, 1990. IL: 8-9+.

———. *Betty Crocker's New International Cookbook.* New York: Prentice-Hall, 1989. IL: 8-9+.

Davis, Barbara. *Learning Science and Metric through Cooking.* New York: Sterling Publishing Co., 1977. IL: 4-7.

Denny, Roz. *A Taste of Britain.* New York: Thomson Learning, 1994. IL: 4-7.

———. *A Taste of China.* New York: Thomson Learning, 1994. IL: 4-7.

———. *A Taste of France.* New York: Thomson Learning, 1994. IL: 4-7.

———. *A Taste of India.* New York: Thomson Learning, 1994. IL: 4-7.

Farmer, Fannie. *The Fannie Farmer Cookbook.* New York: Knopf, 1990. IL: 7-9+; RL: 7.

Gaspari, Claudia. *Food in Italy.* Vero Beach, FL: Rourke Publications, 1989. IL: 5-8

George, Jean Craighead. *The Wild, Wild Cookbook: A Guide for Young Food Foragers.* New York: Crowell, 1982. IL: 5-8.

Germaine, Elizabeth, and Ann L. Burckhardt. *Cooking the Australian Way.* Minneapolis, MN: Lerner Publications, 1990. IL: 6-9.

Gomez, Paolo. *Food in Mexico.* Vero Beach, FL: Rourke Publications, 1989. IL: 5-8.

Haines, Gail Kay. *Baking in a Box, Cooking on a Can.* New York: Morrow, 1981. IL: 5-8.

Hargittai, Magdolna. *Cooking the Hungarian Way.* Minneapolis, MN: Lerner Publications, 1986. IL: 6-9.

Harrison, Supenn, and Judy Monroe. *Cooking the Thai Way.* Minneapolis, MN: Lerner Publications, 1986. IL: 6-9.

Henry, Edna. *Native American Cookbook.* New York: Messner, 1983. IL: 6-9.

Hughes, Helga. *Cooking the Austrian Way.* Minneapolis, MN: Lerner Publications, 1990. IL: 6-9.

Hunt, Bernice Kohn. *Easy Gourmet Cooking for Young People and Beginners.* Indianapolis, IN: Bobbs Merrill, 1973. IL: 4-7.

Jackson, Jonathan. *The Teenage Chef: A Young Adult's Guide to Cooking.* New York: Warne, 1983. IL: 7-9+.

Karoff, Barbara. *South American Cooking: Foods and Feasts from the New World.* Reading, MA: Addison-Wesley, 1989. IL: 6-9.

Katzman, Susan Manlin. *For Kids Who Cook: Recipes and Treats.* New York: Holt, Rinehart and Winston, 1977. IL: 6-9.

Kaufman, Cheryl. *Cooking the Caribbean Way.* Minneapolis, MN: Lerner Publications, 1988. IL: 6-9.

Kaur, Sharon. *Food in India.* Vero Beach, FL: Rourke Publications, 1989. IL: 5-8.

Keene, Carolyn. *The Nancy Drew Cookbook: Clues to Good Cooking.* New York: Grosset & Dunlap, 1973. IL: 5-8.

Kenda, Margaret, and Phyllis S. Williams. *Cooking Wizardry for Kids.* New York: Barron's, 1990. IL: 5-7.

Krementz, Jill. *Fun of Cooking.* New York, Knopf, 1985. IL: 4-7; RL: 8.

Kyte, Kathleen Sharar. *In Charge: A Complete Handbook for Kids with Working Parents.* New York: Knopf, 1983. IL: 4-7.

MacDonald, Kate. *Anne of Green Gables Cookbook.* New York: Oxford University Press, 1986. IL: 5-7; RL: 7.

Madavan, Vijay. *Cooking the Indian Way.* Minneapolis, MN: Lerner Publications, 1985. IL: 6-9.

Munsen, Sylvia. *Cooking the Norwegian Way.* Minneapolis, MN: Lerner Publications, 1982. IL: 6-9.

Nabwire, Constance, and Bertha Vining Montgomery. *Cooking the African Way.* Minneapolis, MN: Lerner Publications, 1988. IL: 6-9.

Nathan, Joan. *The Children's Jewish Holiday Kitchen.* New York: Schocken Books, 1987. IL: 4-7.

Nguyen, Chi, and Judy Monroe. *Cooking the Vietnamese Way.* Minneapolis, MN: Lerner Publications, 1985. IL: 6-9.

Osseo-Asare, Fran. *A Good Soup Attracts Chairs: A First African Cookbook for American Kids.* Gretna, LA: Pelican Publishing, 1993. IL: 5-8.

Parnell, Helga. *Cooking the German Way.* Minneapolis, MN: Lerner Publications, 1988. IL: 6-9.

———. *Cooking the South American Way.* Minneapolis, MN: Lerner Publications, 1991. IL: 6-9.

Paul, Aileen. *Kids Cooking Without a Stove: A Cookbook for Young Children.* Garden City, NY: Doubleday, 1975. IL: 4-7.

Penner, Lucille Recht. *The Colonial Cookbook.* New York: Hastings House, 1976. IL: 5-8.

Perl, Lila. *Hunter's Stew and Hangtown Fry: What Pioneer America Ate and Why.* New York: Clarion, 1977. IL: 5-8; RL: 11.

———. *Slumps, Grunts and Snickerdoodles: What Colonial America Ate and Why.* New York: Clarion, 1975. IL: 5-8; RL: 9.

Pfrommer, Marian. *On the Range: Cooking Western Style.* New York: Atheneum, 1981. IL: 5-8.

Pringle, Laurence P. *Wild Foods: A Beginner's Guide to Identifying, Harvesting and Cooking Safe and Tasty Plants from the Outdoors.* New York: Four Winds Press, 1978. IL: 5-8.

Purdy, Susan Gold. *Christmas Cooking around the World.* New York: Watts, 1983. IL: 5-9.

Ridwell, Jenny. *A Taste of Italy.* New York: Thomson Learning, 1994. IL: 4-7.

————. *A Taste of Japan.* New York: Thomson Learning, 1994. IL: 4-7.

Rollband, James. *The Long and the Short of Chinese Cooking.* Trumansburg, NY: Crossing Press, 1976. IL: 7-9+.

Rombauer, Irma, and Marion R. Becker. *The Joy of Cooking.* Indianapolis, IN: Bobbs Merrill, 1975. IL: 7-9+.

Scobey, Joan. *The Fannie Farmer Junior Cookbook.* Boston: Little, Brown, 1993. IL: 4-8.

Scherie, Strom. *Stuffin' Muffin: Muffin Pan Cooking for Kids.* Avon, CT: Young People's Press, 1981. IL: 4-7.

Shapiro, Rebecca. *Whole World of Cooking.* Boston: Little, Brown, 1972. IL: 5-8+.

Steinkoler, Ronnie. *A Jewish Cookbook for Children.* New York: Messner, 1980. IL: 4-7.

Stewart, Jullian. *French Cooking.* New York: Crescent Books, 1992. IL: 6-9.

————. *Italian Cooking.* New York: Crescent Books, 1992. IL: 6-9.

————. *Southwestern Cooking.* New York: Crescent Books, 1992. IL: 6-9.

Tan, Jennifer. *Food in China.* Vero Beach, FL: Rourke Publications, 1989. IL: 6-9.

Torre, Betty L. *It's Easy to Cook: Favorite American Recipes.* Garden City, NY: Doubleday, 1977. IL: 5-8.

Toth, Robin. *Naturally It's Good . . . I Cooked It Myself!* Crozet, VT: Betterway, 1982. IL: 5-7; RL: 7.

Van Cleave, Jill. *Big, Soft Chewy Cookies.* Chicago: Contemporary Books, 1991. IL: 7-9+.

Waldee, Lynne Marie. *Cooking the French Way.* Minneapolis, MN: Lerner Publications, 1982. IL: 6-9.

Walker, Barbara Muhs. *Little House Cookbook: Frontier Foods from Laura Ingalls Wilder's Classic Stories.* New York: HarperCollins, 1979. IL: 4-7; RL: 9.

Warner, Margaret Brink, and Ruth Ann Hayward. *What's Cooking?: Favorite Recipes from Around the World.* Boston: Little, Brown, 1981. IL: 5-8.

Weston, Reiko. *Cooking the Japanese Way.* Minneapolis, MN: Lerner Publications, 1983. IL: 6-9.

Wolfe, Robert L., and Diane Wolfe. *Holiday Cooking Around the World.* Minneapolis, MN: Lerner Publications, 1985. IL: 6-9; RL: 5.

————. *Vegetarian Cooking Around the World.* Minneapolis, MN: Lerner Publications, 1992. IL: 6-9.

Zamojska-Hutchins, Danuta. *Cooking the Polish Way.* Minneapolis, MN: Lerner Publications, 1984. IL: 6-9.

Professional Sources

Demonstration is so common a teaching method, that it figures in most other methods. In some cases it is assumed that all know what a demonstration is. A search of the ERIC database under teaching methods for the term used, the researcher found over 1,000 citiations under the index term, *demonstrations (educational)*. Demonstration is described as "a teaching method in which explanations are given by example or experiment." Related terms include: *demonstration centers, educational laboratories, laboratories,* and *laboratory procedures*. One can also find more information by looking for *modeling, direct instruction,* and *mastery learning*. Demonstration is a powerful method of providing experience to an individual. Its weakness is that it concentrates on the learning of procedures rather than on theory or transfer of knowledge to other situations.

There are many articles on this subject, and the demonstration as a process can be found in most teaching methods sources. The following list of articles provides a fair sampling.

Allen, Ralph. "You Can Get Them To Believe Just About Anything." *Science Activities* 12, no. 2 (March-April 1975), pp. 30-31.

Bandura, A. *Social Learning Theory*. Englewood Cliffs, NJ: Prentice-Hall, 1977.

Five Dimensions of Demonstration. Norman, OK: Teacher Corps Research Adaptation Cluster, University of Oklahoma Press, 1977.

Garrett, R. M., and I. F. Roberts. "Demonstration Versus Small Group Practical Work in Science Education. A Critical Review of Studies Since 1900. *Studies in Science Education* 9 (1982), pp. 109-46.

Gropper, George Leonard. *The Representational Role of Demonstrations in Teaching Concepts and Principles in Science: Studies in Televised Instruction, Dimensions of Visual Representation*. Pittsburgh, PA: Metropolitan Pittsburgh Educational Television Station and American Institutes for Research, 1966.

Kemp, Jerrold E. *National Workshop on Educational Media Demonstrations. Final Report*. San Jose, CA: San Jose State College Press, 1962.

Lightfoot, Donald. "Using Video Cassette Demonstrations in the Biochemistry Laboratory." *Journal of Chemical Education* 55, no. 12 (December 1978), pp. 786-87.

Mittler, Gene A. "Instructional Strategies in Art Education: A Closer Look." *School Arts* 93, no. 3 (November 1993), pp. 38-40.

Putnam, Joyce, and Betty Johns. *Potential of Demonstration Teaching in Teacher Preparation and Staff Development Programs. Research and Evaluation in Teacher Education: Program Evaluation Series No. 14*. Lansing, MI: College of Education, Michigan State University, 1987. ED 280845.

Rivera, Diane M., and Deborah D. Smith. "Influence of Modeling on Acquisition and Generalization of Computational Skills: A Summary of Research Findings from Three Sites." *Learning Disability Quarterly* 10, no. 1 (Winter 1987), pp. 69-80.

Rivera, Diane M., and Deborah Deutsch Smith. "Using a Demonstration Strategy to Teach Midschool Students with Learning Disabilities How to Compute Long Division." *Journal of Learning Disabilities* 21, no. 2 (February 1988), pp. 77-81.

Wise, Beth S. *Modeling: A Direct Instruction Model for Programming Reading Comprehension.* Paper presented at the annual meeting of Texas State Council of the International Reading Association, Dallas, TX, March 14-16, 1985. ED 258161.

Womack, Sid T. "Modes of Instruction: Expository, Demonstration, Inquiry, Individualized." *Clearing House* 62, no. 5 (January 1989), pp. 205-10.

Zimmerman, Barry J., and Arnold Jaffe. "Teaching Through Demonstration: The Effects of Structuring, Imitation, and Age." *Journal of Educational Psychology* 69, no. 6 (December 1977), pp. 773-78.

6

Descriptive Writing

INTRODUCTION

P ersons, scenes, places, settings, and events pictured through writing are defined as descriptive writing or text. Description is usually embedded in other types of writing, because it supports the purposes of these other forms. In fact, it is crucial to all other forms. Narrative, persuasive, procedural, and argumentative writing flounder or fail without well-written description. Its use provides background and concrete information or detail which allows the reader to believe the author.

Descriptive writing relies on the five senses and the ability to observe and convey sensory details about persons, places, objects, or events. It is through sight, smell, sound, taste, speech, and the kinesthetic behavior that human beings respond to their environment. The concrete details distinguish one person, place, thing, and event from another and become significant as identifiers. The careful selection of words that describe these details communicate the author's perceptions and address the audience's needs. With audience perception and understanding, the author's message is experienced as accurately as possible.

Descriptive writing often includes long sentences and complicated structure. Active verbs and vivid adjectives, as well as adverbial clauses, are inherent to the semantics. For descriptions of people, the reader might expect to find adjectives that distinguish one character as distinct from another. The author's point of view or judgment is often shared, whether or not it is intentional. It is in description that the reader most often finds subtle stereotypes and bias or strong opinions. Because the author's purpose is to convey an idea of concept, use of similes and metaphors to describe certain characteristics are common. Well-described images portrayed in short anecdotes convey the essence of the character, especially if the reader is likely to have experienced something or someone of a similar description. Places are also described with adjectives and phrases. Prepositional phrases clarify and vitalize the content and may evoke emotion. Description is often difficult to write and read because the main idea or meaning must be inferred by the reader at levels of prior knowledge and experience different from the author's.

Descriptive writing appears as a pure form at times (Figure 7). In such instances it has unusual appeal to some young people. Many adolescents are eager to experience the world on their own without parents or authorities intruding. They want to compare their own feelings to those of others, and poetry, especially descriptive poetry, is one means of doing so. Escape or journeying can be experienced in travel guides or in the travel and survival stories found in the travel sections of library media collections. Travel guides are used for planning family vacations or dreaming about other places. The descriptions used in catalogs of things treasured or valued by young people can make them figuratively drool. Descriptive catalogs for just about every commodity are delivered to American homes daily. While some catalogs include descriptions that become persuasive ads, many are just straight

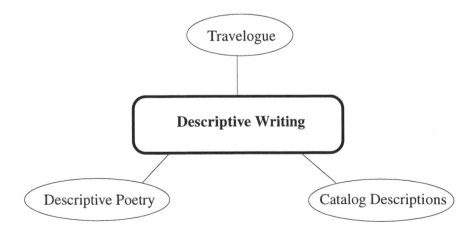

Figure 7. Descriptive Forms

description. Such descriptive writing serves as a powerful advertising tool. One need only look at the descriptive listings in videotape, audiotape, CD, and clothing catalogs for examples. It is the appeal to the senses and the selection of detail that will be the motivators.

Professional Sources

Print

Most of the sources suggested here provide evidence of the skill that is required for students to infer and gather meaning from descriptive writing. A good descriptive passage actually enhances comprehension if the student connects it with prior knowledge, and if the strength of the appeal to the senses and emotions is strong.

Acton, Karen. *Imagery: Activity Guide.* Cedar Falls, IA: Iowa Area Education Agency 7, 1980. ED 239203.

Alvermann, Donna. "The Compensatory Effect of Graphic Organizers on Descriptive Text." *Journal of Educational Research* 75, no. 1 (September-October 1981), pp. 44-48.

Bean, Ariel Storey. *A Descriptive Study of Creative Writing at the Junior High School Level.* Doctoral dissertation, Brigham Young University, 1974. University Microfilms No. 74-27,520. ED 101347.

Bloom, Lynn Z. "Actions Speak Louder . . . ." *Exercise Exchange* 22, no. 1 (Fall 1977), pp. 46-47.

Boiarsky, Carolyn. "Free Writing—When More Is Less." *Today's Education* 69, no. 3 (September-October 1980), pp. 39-41.

Brittain, Norman A., ed. 1969. *Writing Description and Narration.* New York: Holt, Rinehart and Winston.

Carrell, Patricia L. "Reading and Writing Descriptive and Persuasive Texts." *Modern Language Journal* 75, no. 3 (Fall 1991), pp. 314-24.

Engberg, Norwa J. "Observation and Order in the Writing of Description." *Exercise Exchange* 20, no. 2 (Spring 1976), pp. 10-14.

Kurth, Anita. "Birds and Dragons: An Exercise in Descriptive Writing." *Exercise Exchange* 32, no. 1 (Fall 1986), pp. 27-28.

Kurylo, Lynne. "Language for Seeing: Using Objects to Teach Speaking and Writing Skills." *TESL Talk* 11, no. 2 (Spring 1980), pp. 16-21.

O'Mahony, John F. "Development of Person Description Over Adolescence" *Journal of Youth and Adolescence* 15, no. 5 (October 1986), pp. 389-403.

Piolat, Annie, and Jean-Yves Roussey. "Narrative and Descriptive Text Revising Strategies and Procedures." *European Journal of Psychology of Education* 6, no. 2 (June 1991), pp. 155-63.

Smith, Elaine Campbell. "Simile Darn You Simile." *Elementary English* 49, no. 4 (April 1972), pp. 585-86.

Stancil, Genise A. *Descriptive Writing Unit*. Washington, DC: District of Columbia Public Schools, 1973. ED 096646.

Taylor, Michael. "Draw: A Heuristic for Expressive Writing." *Journal of Teaching Writing* 4, no. 2 (Fall 1985), pp. 210-14.

Walling, Donovan R. "Sense Exploration and Descriptive Writing: A Practical Exercise." *Exercise Exchange* 23, no. 1 (Fall 1978), pp. 30-34.

Wolfe, Don M. "Crucial First Assignment: Describing a Room." *Elementary English* 47, no. 6 (October 1970), pp. 784-86.

Nonprint

Creative Writing: A Unit of Study. Niles, IL: United Learning, 1984. 4 sound filmstrips.

Schrank, Jeffrey. *Right and Lively: The Art of Descriptive Writing*. Palatine, IL: Learning Seed Co., 1977. 75 slides, 1 sound cassette, 2 spirit masters, 1 teacher's guide, geometric forms cards.

Skeel, Dorothy J., ed. 1971. *Developing Creative Ability*. South Holland, IL: H. Wilson Company. 2 sound recordings.

DESCRIPTIVE POETRY

An impression, a written perception passed on by the author or poet, an image evoked by words or phrases in poetic form—these are definitions of descriptive poetry. The poet uses rhythm, rhyme, meter, words, and all other devices to recollect some natural scene, object, or event. All of the senses and movement are brought to bear in the memories elicited. Objects become more than the concrete items themselves because of the poet's interpretation and description of related images and thoughts.

The reader might expect to encounter vivid nouns and very active verbs supported with adjectives in poetic forms. Such writing relies heavily on the background of the reader and requires selective interpretation and creative imaging.

While the appeal of descriptive poetry is often stereotyped, it is easily shared with students. It can be a form that moves any sense or emotion that the adolescent is experiencing. Poetry is found in many "non-standard" places. Often it touches the essence of what may be on the mind of a young person. When free to read and browse, students often find just the words that describe their own feelings or ideas. Descriptive poetry is an emotional dance of words.

Professional Sources

The sources listed here include indexes for locating descriptive poetry and methods books that include suggestions for writing descriptive poetry. There are a plethora of books on poetry. The ones listed here are representative of the kinds of sources that might prove valuable in locating materials and ideas.

Print

Indexes and References

Blackburn III, G. Meredith. *Index to Poetry for Children and Young People: 1982-1987.* New York: H. W. Wilson, 1989.

Brewton, John E., and Sara W. Brewton. *Index to Children's Poetry.* New York: H. W. Wilson, 1942.

———. *Index to Children's Poetry, First Supplement.* New York: H. W. Wilson, 1954.

———. *Index to Children's Poetry, Second Supplement.* New York: H. W. Wilson, 1965.

Brewton, John E., Sara W. Brewton, and G. Meredith Blackburn, III. *Index to Poetry for Children and Young People: 1964-1969.* New York: H. W. Wilson, 1972.

Brewton, John E., G. Meredith Blackburn, III, and Lorraine A. Blackburn. *Index to Poetry for Children and Young People: 1970-1975.* New York: H. W. Wilson, 1978.

———. *Index to Poetry for Children and Young People: 1976-1981.* New York: H. W. Wilson, 1984.

Chapman, Dorothy Hilton. *Index to Poetry by Black American Women.* Westport, CT: Greenwood Press, 1986.

The Columbia Granger's World of Poetry. New York: Columbia University Press, 1991.

Hazen, Edith P., and Dorothy Fryer. *The Columbia Granger's Index to Poetry.* New York: Columbia University Press, 1990.

Hoffman, Herbert J., and Rita Ludwig Hoffman. *International Index to Recorded Poetry.* New York: H. W. Wilson, 1983.

Katz, William A., and Linda Sternberg Katz. *The Columbia Granger's Guide to Poetry Anthologies.* New York: Columbia University Press, 1991.

Kline, Victoria. *Last Lines: An Index to the Last Lines of Poetry.* New York: Facts on File, 1991.

Master Index to Poetry: An Index to Poetry in Anthologies and Collections. Great Neck, NY: Poetry Index Press, 1988.

Olexer, Marycile. *Poetry Anthologies for Children and Young People.* Chicago: American Library Association, 1985.

Poetry Index Annual: A Title, Author, First Line and Subject Index to Poetry in Anthologies. Great Neck, NY: Roth Publishing, 1982-. Annual.

Subject Index to Poetry for Children and Young People, 1957-1975. Chicago: American Library Association, 1977.

Teaching Methods

Anderson, Edward. *Positive Use of Rap Music in the Classroom.* Virginia: 1993. ED 353588.

Carpenter, John. *Creating the World: Poetry, Art, and Children.* Seattle, WA: University of Washington Press, 1986.

Couch, Lezlie Laws. "So Much Depends On How You Begin: A Poetry Lesson." *English Journal* 76, no. 7 (November 1987), pp. 29-35.

Hansen, I. V., et al. "Poetry and the Visual Arts." *English in Australia* 60 (June 1982), pp. 19-31.

Hollman, Marilyn J. "From Art to Poetry: 'Prance as They Dance.' " *English Journal* 78, no. 3 (May 1989), pp. 24-27.

Larrick, Nancy. *Let's Do a Poem!: Introducing Poetry to Children through Listening, Singing, Chanting, Impromptu Choral Reading, Body Movement, Dance, and Dramatization, Including 98 Favorite Songs and Poems.* New York: Delacorte, 1991.

McFarlane, Peter. "Making Meaning: A Teaching Approach to the Poetry of Wilfred Owen Using Visual and Performing Arts." *English in Australia* 81 (1987), pp. 4-14.

Parsons, Les. *Poetry, Themes and Activities: Exploring the Fun and Fantasy of Language.* Portsmouth, NH: Heinemann, 1992.

Pica, Rae. *Poetry in Motion: Poems and Activities for Moving and Learning with Young Children.* Byron, CA: Front Row Experience, 1986.

Segreto, Anna. "Teachers, Leave Those Kids Alone." *Journal of Teaching Writing* 8, no. 1 (Spring-Summer 1989), pp. 31-39.

Smith, Richard. *Using Poetry to Teach Reading and Language Arts: A Handbook for Elementary School Teachers.* New York: Teachers College Press, 1984.

Thomas, Lorenzo. "You've Got to Put Yourself in It: The Voice of Poetry." *Teachers and Writers* 22, no. 3 (January-February 1991), pp. 13-15.

Walter, Nina Willis. *Let Them Write Poetry: A Book about the Teaching of Poetry Appreciation through the Writing of Poetry for Teachers of Children from Kindergarten through High School.* New York: Holt, Rinehart and Winston, 1962.

Weber, Elizabeth C. *Guidelines for Children's Poetry Appreciation and Poetry Writing and Suggested Books and Activities.* Paper presented at the annual meeting of the International Reading Association, San Antonio, TX, April 26-30, 1993. ED 357332.

Wetherall, Nancy B. "Leonard Cohen: Poems Set to Music." *English Journal* 62, no. 4 (April 1973), pp. 551-55.

Wilson, Raymond. "The Tone Poem." *Use of English* 35, no. 2 (Spring 1984), pp. 57-63.

Womack, Nancy. *Teaching Poetry to Adolescents: Nine Principles Plus One.* 1975. ED 128807.

Databases on CD-ROM

For full information and requirements, check *CD-ROMS in Print:* Meckler Annual. Poetry indexes are now also available through the Internet. For such databases, check Internet guides.

Columbia Granger's World of Poetry on CD-ROM. New York: Columbia University Press, 1994. MS-DOS.

The English Poetry Full-Text Database. Cambridge, England: Chadwyck-Healey, 1992. MS-DOS.

Poem Finder on Disc. Great Neck, NY: Roth Publishing, 1991. MS-DOS.

Poetry in Motion. Santa Monica, CA: Voyager, 1992. Macintosh.

Nonprint

Poems as Description. Washington, DC: WETV-TV; Springfield, VA: Children's Television International, 1976. 15 min. 1 videocassette.

Poetry Explained by Karla Kuskin. Weston, CT: Weston Woods, 1980. 1 sound filmstrip.

Activity: Dance and Creative Movement to Poetry

Inner Chimes: Poems on Poetry (Boyds Mill Press, 1992), selected by Bobbye S. Goldstein and illustrated by Jane Breskin Zalben, is a wonderful choice for introducing this activity. Each poem in the volume was selected to express the fun of listening to, reading, and writing poetry. The choices are exceptional. Almost all the poems are examples of what descriptive poetry is. Choices range from Eve Merriam's verse about poems, "an inner chime that makes you want to/Tap your feet or swerve in a curve" to Naoshi Koriyama's statement "One is not amazed,/At first glance,/By a poem,/ Which is as tight-closed/As a tiny bud." Use the poetry to help students think about how poets describe things around them. More traditional examples of descriptive poems follow:

"Spring" by William Shakespeare
"To Spring" by William Blake

"Pippa's Song" by Robert Browning

"Dust of Snow" by Robert Frost

"The Eagle" by Alfred, Lord Tennyson

"Ode to the West Wind" by Percy Bysshe Shelley

"Cavalry Crossing a Ford" by Walt Whitman

"Dreams" by Langston Hughes

"Reflections Dental" by Phyllis McGinley

"Seal" by William Jay Smith

For other poems, have students browse through poetry books and make their own choices. Poems from Lillian Morrison's *The Break Dance Kids: Poems of Sport, Motion, and Locomotion* (Lothrop, Lee and Shepard, 1985) is also a good choice for introducing this activity. Discuss with the class the metaphor of poetry as dance.

Following the poetry exchange, use videotaped examples of creative dance and expression. What does dance have in common with the poems selected? If the students are especially interested in pursuing music as poetry, think about using the film *He Makes Me Feel Like Dancin'* (Direct Cinema Limited, 1983), which captures Jacques d'Amboise teaching students how to dance. Other good possibilities are *Ailey Dances* (ABC Video Enterprises, 1982), a taped performance by a dance company; and programs from the instructional television series, *Arts Alive* (AIT, 1984), such as "Elements of Dance" and "Creating Dance." These video programs help students visualize the concept that dance movement manipulates space, time, and energy to express emotion or reflect an idea or story.

After viewing the video performances, discuss with students how the moving or dancing body is similar to the poet's use of words to express emotion or to describe the world around us. Dancing is part of the adolescent experience, and this activity will allow the teacher to expand on the experience; recommend to students that they try dance and reading verbal expression together. The challenge to students is how they might combine descriptive poetry about a topic of interest with music and creative dance or movement.

Because some students are likely to be reluctant, focus on topics of interest to them, anything from love to nature. The dances may range from simple movements identified with the help of the physical education teacher to more complicated dance steps. Anyone who has watched Rap artists or MTV will realize that many students, given even slight encouragement, will find ways for expressing themselves in movement. Encourage students to consider how one can move the arms, hands, feet, head, and whole body as a means of self-expression.

The teacher and library media specialist may model a process for brainstorming a topic, locating poems and music, and choreographing dance movements with their finds. Assist students in brainstorming a topic on their own. After one or two topics have been identified, the students may begin their search for poems. Ask the library media specialist to introduce students to poetry indexes or suggest that students browse through the poetry section of the library (Dewey Decimal Classification numbers 811 or 821). If students have a hard time getting started, suggest that they collect the poems that they consider descriptive of nature, a particular place, or a specific kind of weather, such as snow. A poem such as "Snow Toward Evening" by Melville Cane in *Snow Toward Evening: A Year in a River Valley,* edited by Josette Frank and illustrated by Thomas Locker (Dial, 1990) would be an excellent poem to work with if a student chose snow as a topic. The library media specialist might use picture book volumes of poetry to help the visualization process.

Poetry indexes might be searched by topic to see what and how much is available. A check with the teacher at this point will be useful to make sure that students are on target with their selections. As students select their poems, they may associate a mood or type of music with them. An assortment of music cassettes or CDs on hand would be helpful. Assist students in determining what music would best correspond to the poems they have selected. Encourage them to read each poem aloud and think about what kinds of body movements come to mind to express the poet's message. These activities are likely to be done in concert as students select a poem and find music that might work. The students will sense success as they begin to add movement.

The next step is the actual choreographing of the dance to the chosen music. Students need to decide how they will share the poetry, music, and dance: for example, some students could move to the music as another student reads the poem slowly, or the music might be played softly in the background as the poem is read, then more music added as the mood is dramatized.

The students may enjoy performing their pieces with others live or on video. It is sure to bring descriptive poetry to life.

Student Sources

Student sources of descriptive poetry are so extensive that only an example of one specific area can be included here. The following is a list of illustrated children's books on nature and weather.

Adoff, Arnold. *Tornado! Poems*. New York: Delacorte, 1977.

Atwood, Ann. *Fly with the Wind, Flow with the Water*. New York: Scribner's, 1979.

Booth, David, ed. 1990. *Voices on the Wind: Poems for All Seasons*. New York: Morrow.

Butler, Beverly. *The Wind and Me*. New York: Dodd, Mead, 1971.

Fisher, Aileen Lucia. *Up, Up the Mountain*. New York: T. Y. Crowell Co., 1968.

Hollander, John. *Wind and the Rain*. Garden City, NY: Doubleday, 1961.

Lewis, Richard. *In the Night, Still Dark*. New York: Atheneum, 1988.

————. *The Wind and the Rain: Children's Poems*. New York: Simon & Schuster, 1968.

Lindbergh, Reeve. *Grandfather's Lovesong*. New York: Viking, 1993.

Mizumura, Kazue. *Flower, Moon, Snow: A Book of Haiku*. New York: T.Y. Crowell Co., 1977.

Prelutsky, Jack. *It's Snowing! It's Snowing!* New York: Greenwillow Books, 1984.

————. *Rainy Rainy Saturday*. New York: Greenwillow Books, 1980.

Sky-Peck, Kathryn, ed. 1991. *Who Has Seen the Wind?: An Illustrated Collection of Poetry for Young People*. New York: Rizzoli.

Southey, Robert. *The Cataract of Lodore: A Poem*. New York: Dial Books for Young Readers, 1991.

Yolen, Jane, ed. 1993. *Weather Report*. Honesdale, PA: Boyds Mills Press/ Wordsong.

Weygant, Noemi. *It's Winter!* Philadelphia, PA: Westminster Press, 1969.

Professional Sources

The use of dance and movement for self-expression creates a strong link between the arts and physical education or movement education. The suggestions that follow provide definition, reference, and background in the use of dance in other subject areas as well as information about dance as a method to increase cognition and appreciation.

Print

Reference and Theory Books

Adamczyk, Alice J. *Black Dance: An Annotated Bibliography*. New York: Garland, 1989.

Adshead, Janet. *The Study of Dance*. London: Dance Books, 1981.

Alison, Lee. *A Handbook of Creative Dance and Drama*. Portsmouth, NH: Heineman, 1991.

Bibliographic Guide to Dance. Boston: G. K. Hall. Annual.

Clarke, Mary, and David Vaughn. *Encyclopedia of Dance and Ballet*. New York: Putnam, 1977.

DeVaney, Margaret T., and Phyllis A. Penney, eds. 1986. *The Dance Directory: Programs of Professional Preparation in American Colleges and Universities.* Reston, VA: American Alliance for Health, Physical Education, Recreation, and Dance.

Docherty, David. *Education through Dance Experience.* Bellingham, WA: Educational Designs and Consultants, 1975. ED 129834.

Furst, Clara, and Mildred Rockefeller. *The Effective Dance Program in Physical Education.* West Nyack, NY: Parker Publishing, 1981.

Gilbert, Anne Green. *Creative Dance for All Ages: A Conceptual Approach.* Reston, VA: American Alliance for Health, Physical Education, Recreation and Dance, 1992. ED 355182.

————. "Dance: A Nonverbal Approach to Learning the Three Rs." *Journal of Physical Education and Recreation* 50, no. 9 (November-December 1979), pp. 58-60.

Gray, Judith Anne. *Dance Instruction: Science Applied to the Art of Movement.* Champaign, IL: Human Kinetics Books, 1989.

Leung, Katherine. *Facilitating Speech, Language and Auditory Training through Tap Dancing and Creative Movement.* Paper presented at the annual convention for the Council of Exceptional Children, New Orleans, LA, March 31-April 4, 1986.

Logan, Moira. "Dance in the Schools: A Personal Account." *Theory into Practice* 23, no. 4 (Fall 1984), pp. 300-302.

Koegler, Horst, ed. 1987. *The Concise Oxford Dictionary of Ballet.* New York: Oxford.

Martyn, Laurel. *Let Them Dance: A Preparation for Dance and Life.* London: Dance Books, 1985.

Metheny, Eleanor. *Moving and Knowing in Sport, Dance, Physical Education: A Collection of Speeches.* Mountain View, CA: Peek Publications, 1975.

Pease, Esther Elizabeth. *Modern Dance.* Dubuque, IA: W. C. Brown Co., 1976.

Preston-Dunlop, Valerie. *A Handbook for Dance in Education.* London: Macdonald and Evans, 1984.

Robertson, Allen, and Donald Hutrea. *The Dance Handbook.* Boston: G. K. Hall, 1990.

Tanner, Patricia, and Kate Barret. "Movement Education: What Does It Mean?" *Journal of Physical Education and Recreation* 46, no. 4 (April 1975), pp. 19-20.

Teaching Methods

Akenson, James E. "Linkages of Art and Social Studies: Focus on Modern Dance." *Theory and Research in Social Education* 19, no. 1 (Winter 1991), pp. 95-108.

Aldrich, Kenneth B. "'Rhythm, Movement and Synchrony' Effective Teaching Tools." *Journal of Physical Education, Recreation and Dance* 60, no. 4 (April 1989), pp. 91-94.

Cohan, Robert. *The Dance Workshop: A Guide to the Fundamentals of Movement.* New York: Simon & Schuster, 1986.

Dance: Creative/Rhymthic Movement Education. A Conceptual Approach for K-12 Curriculum Development. Madison, WI: Wisconsin State Department of Education, 1981. ED 213707.

D'Auboise, Jacques, Hope Cook, and Carolyn George. *Teaching the Magic of Dance.* New York: Simon and Schuster, 1983.

Exiner, Johanna, and Phyllis Lloyd. *Teaching Creative Movement.* Boston: Plays, Inc., 1974.

Guest, Ann Hutchinson. *Your Move: A New Approach to the Study of Movement and Dance.* New York: Gordon and Breach, 1983.

Heausler, Nancy L. *Teaching Language Skills Using Dance/Movement Methods.* Paper presented at the annual meeting of the Mid-South Educational Research Association, Mobile, AL, November 11-13, 1987. ED 296307.

Hypes, Jeanette. *Discover Dance: Teaching Modern Dance in Secondary Schools.* Washington, DC: National Dance Association, 1978.

Leese, Sue, and Moira Packer. *Creative Dance for Schools.* Boston: Plays, Inc., 1981.

Marx, Ellen. "Poetry and Movement." *Journal of Physical Education and Recreation* 47, no. 3 (March 1976), pp. 70-71.

Nahumcl, Nadia Chilkovsky. *Dance Curriculum-Resource Guide: Comprehensive Dance Education for Secondary Schools.* New York: American Dance Guild, 1980.

Sandoval, Sylvia Mocroft. "The Seasons: Nature Imagery in Dance." *Teachers and Writers Magazine* 12, no. 3 (Spring 1981), pp. 14-19.

Smith, Karen Lynn. "Dance and Imagery - The Link between Movement and Imagination." *Journal of Physical Education, Recreation and Dance* 61, no. 2 (February 1990), pp. 17-32.

Tramwell, Peggy. "Poetry and Dance for Children." *Journal of Physical Education, Recreation and Dance* 53, no. 7 (October 1982), pp. 75-76.

Weikart, Phyllis S. *Teaching Movement and Dance: A Sequential Approach to Rhymthic Movement.* Ypsilanti, MI: High/Scope Press, 1982.

Weiler, Virginia Bryant, et al. *A Guide to Curriculum Planning in Dance.* Madison, WI: Wisconsin Department of Education, 1988. ED 305349.

Wiener, Jack, and John Lidstone. *Creative Movement for Children: A Dance Program for the Classroom.* New York: Van Nostrand, 1969.

Nonprint

Ailey Dances. Long Branch, NJ: Kulture/ABC Video Enterprises in association with James Lipton Productions, 1982. 85 min. 1 videocassette.

Arts Alive: Creating Dance. Bloomington, IN: AIT, 1984. 15 min. 1 videocassette.

Arts Alive: Elements of Dance. Bloomington, IN: AIT, 1984. 15 min. 1 videocassette.

Dance. Chicago: Encyclopaedia Britannica Educational Corp., 1980. 4 min. One 16mm film.

Discovering Your Expressive Body: Basic Concepts in Dance Training Utilizing Bartenieff Fundamentals. Pennington, NJ: Dance Horizons Video, 1989. 59 min. 1 videocassette.

Dream of Wild Horses. New York: Contemporary Films/McGraw-Hill. 9 Min. One 16mm film.

He Makes Me Feel Like Dancin'. Los Angeles: Direct Cinema Limited, 1983. 51 min. 1 videocassette.

Associations

There are a number of associations concentrating on dance and movement education. The following are two examples. Consult the index of *The Encyclopedia of Associations* (Gale Research Annual) for further information.

National Dance Association
1900 Association Drive
Reston, VA 22091

American Alliance for Health, Physical Education, Recreation and Dance
1900 Association Drive
Reston, VA 22091

TRAVELOGUE

Many adults' favorite pastime consists of daydreaming about places where they would rather be. Other people read and plan trips that they sometimes do not have the time, money, or opportunity to take. Students, too, like to daydream, and many develop the wanderlust early. Finding out about new places can be an exciting pastime.

An old but still popular writing form for learning about other places is the travelogue. A travelogue traditionally is a lecture in which an individual describes his or her travels; the lecture is often accompanied by pictures or slides. Sometimes travelogues take the form of videotapes or travel films. Book or print versions that describe travels abound. In fact, writing about travel is a long established form of writing, as evidenced by the early adventures of Marco Polo. Today, scores of people write for travel magazines. Relative to the travelogue is the travel guidebook, which lists places to visit with commentary in the form of description.

The main purpose of guidebooks and travelogues is the description of a place. The audience varies, but the purpose seldom does. In such writing, the reader expects to find an abundance of descriptive words and phrases.

Adverbs and adjectives become particularly important. The reader's ability to understand analogies and the possession of a varied and large vocabulary is helpful. The organization of travelogues can vary, but most obtain order from the sequence of the journey itself. Places and scenes are described in the order in which they are encountered. Language ranges from simple locational sentence structures to more advanced levels of abstractions, in which the writer may find that a scene reminds him of, or suggests, more lofty ideals. In such writing, the reader will find the devices of descriptive comparison—metaphor and simile.

Travel sources are available in major libraries. Rows of materials may be located in most bookstores. In the past few years, guides for younger readers have become available.

Professional Sources

Print

Bryant, Paul T. *Nature Writing: Giving Students' Writing a Usable Tradition.* Paper presented at the annual meeting of the Conference on College Composition and Communication, Washington, DC, March 13-15, 1980. ED 189647.

Casewit, Curtis W. *How To Make Money from Travel Writing.* Old Saybrook, CT: Globe Pequot Press, 1988.

Crichton, Jean. "Travel USA." *Publishers Weekly* 237 (May 4, 1990), pp. 17-28.

Dodd, Philip, ed. 1982. *The Art of Travel: Essays on Travel Writing.* London: F. Cass.

Frank, Peter. *The Travelogues: 1971-1977.* Los Angeles: Sun and Moon Press, 1982.

Frazier, Ian, et al. *They Went West: The Art and Craft of Travel Writing.* Boston: Houghton Mifflin, 1991.

Going Places: The Guide to Travel Guides. Cambridge, MA: Harvard Common Press, 1989.

Marsden-Smedley, Philip, and Jeffrey Klinke. *Views from Abroad: The Spectator Book of Travel Writing.* Santa Barbara, CA: ISIS Largeprint, 1989.

Murray, John A. *Wild Africa: Three Centuries of Nature Writing from Africa.* New York: Oxford University Press, 1993.

Natarella, Margaret A. "The United States: A Historical Travelogue." *Language Arts* 53, no. 1 (January 1976), pp. 34-36.

Ogden, C. Richard. *Writer's and Photographer's Guide: Travel, Leisure, Sports, Outdoors, Nature.* San Francisco, CA: Clarence House, 1979.

Otness, Harold. "Travel Guidebooks: A World of Information for Libraries." *Wilson Library Bulletin* 67, no. 5 (January 1993), pp. 38-40, 116-117.

Pratt, Mary Louise. *Imperial Eyes: Travel Writing and Transculturation.* New York: Routledge, 1992.

Purcell, Ann, and Carl Purcell. *A Guide to Travel Writing and Photography.* Cincinnati, OH: Writers Digest Books, 1991.

Simony, Maggy, ed. 1987. *The Traveler's Reading Guide: Ready-Made Reading Lists for the Armchair Traveler.* New York: Facts on File.

Society of American Travel Writers. *Travel and Writing and the Two Rs.* Norfolk, VA: The Society of American Travel Writers, 1965.

Taylor, Nancy. *The Travel Journal: An Assessment Tool for Overseas Study.* New York: Council for International Educational Exchange, 1991. ED 331046.

Wood, Larry. "Is Travel Writing a Growing Profession?" *Journalism Quarterly* 54, no. 4 (Winter 1977), pp. 761-64.

Zobel, Louise Purwin. *The Travel Writer's Handbook.* Cincinnati, OH: Writers Digest Books, 1984.

Associations

Society of American Travel Writers
1120 Connecticut Avenue, NW Suite 940
Washington, DC 20036

Activity: Slide/Tape Production

Slide/tape production has been selected for this activity because slides are easy to manipulate. Most schools still have slide projectors. The activity can also be done by editing a videotape. Those with access to a computer are in a position to develop a slide/tape presentation on screen. Many photography labs are now able to produce photographs on computer disk or CD-ROM.

Tell the class to imagine that they will be traveling to a special place. Ask: How can you bring back some of your feelings and impressions? How can you share or describe to your friends the things that you have seen, the smells, the tastes, the feelings, the action? Help students explore a number of print and nonprint travel guides and travelogues before you ask them to begin a project of their own. Display books and tapes to be used as resources.

At the beginning of the activity introduce the concept of a travelogue. Using fifteen or twenty scenes from a place you have visited, show the students a chronology or topical arrangement of slides that describe the events shown. Give students an opportunity to share a memorable visit of their own. Suggest that visits to local places can be as exciting as visits to more exotic lands.

Encourage students either to write about a pretend trip to a place they have read about or to make up a travelogue about a place they have actually visited. Consider giving students a prepared list of places to read about before beginning on their "trip."

Checklist

Collect the necessary equipment:

• 35mm camera
• appropriate camera lenses
• slide film (color)
• tripod
• plans for shooting pictures

Research the place to be visited:

Read guides that tell about the place to be visited. While reading the guides, pay attention to the descriptions of specific locations. What is there? What makes the place interesting to travelers? What appeals to you?

Locate information on local maps and atlases, in phonebooks, travel guides, and history sources. Choose some sites to visit. Determine how to get there. Think about what you are going to encounter, who lives there, what the people are like, what words to use to describe the places (verbs and adjectives).

Anticipate scenes that might be shot and how they would be described in words. Make a list of what kinds of things it would be interesting to see, even though there may be surprises along the way. Be aware of the number and variety of pictures that are possible. Plan or anticipate the kind of shots that might be taken. Think about what scenes might require close-ups. Think about the time of day you will be visiting and the lighting that will be available. Prepare a blank form to record and describe shots taken.

Shot #	Date	Site Details (Descriptive Words)	History or Background

Take this opportunity to introduce students to the rudiments of good photography. Review photographs that show close-ups, long-distance shots, and the effects of good lighting. Remind students that it is sometimes a good idea to photograph more than one view of an object or place. Not all pictures turn out well.

After students return from their trips and have their film developed, the work of sorting out the best begins. If students have taken color slides, they can be shown how to use a light table or light box to view the results. Ask them to select from the photos the best views and label the slides by referring to the log they kept. The slides should be laid out in the order they were shot. Then a logical order of presentation may be determined. It can be chronological, functional, or topical.

Usually a slide tape script is written before shooting film. In the case of the travelogue, the students may write from the result of their developed slides. They will be showing the slides in the logical order selected. The students may write the description of the slides. They may think about and describe the highpoints of the experience. Again, details from the log will be useful. Encourage students to practice presenting their descriptions and either memorize or tape record them before they show the slides to their classmates.

Student Sources

Access to travelogues, either written or visual, will vary. Most public libraries include videotapes in their collections. Students need only check under *travelogues* or *travel guides* for information. Or, they may locate the name of a given place and add *-description and travel, -guidebooks,* or *-directories* when they search for the place. Some other possible search terms are *adventure, adventures,* or *journey.*

An example of an audiovisual travelogue is *America's Favorite Places* (Camp Connell, CA: Lark Productions, 1992), 87 min., 1 videocassette.

Print sources will vary. Travelogues and travel stories for adolescents are usually found in the library media center under the Dewey Decimal Classification sections 910 through 919. Many books written for adults are also suitable for the younger readers, especially if they are motivated. The examples provided are similar to autobiographies because they include the author's experiences and describe the events in chronological order as might be found in a diary. However, their purpose is to describe the terrain, the land, the people, and the journey. The writing is more description than narrative.

Clarke, Thurston. *Equator: A Journey*. New York: Morrow, 1988.

Cordell, Michael. *Red Express: The Greatest Rail Journey--From the Berlin Wall to the Great Wall of China*. New York: Prentice-Hall, 1991.

De Villiers, Marq. *Down the Volga: A Journey Through Mother Russia in a Time of Troubles*. New York: Viking, 1992.

Dodwell, Christina. *A Traveller in China*. New York: Beaufort Books, 1986.

Ellis, Jerry. *Walking the Trail: One Man's Journey Along the Trail of Tears*. New York: Delacorte, 1991.

Houston, Dick. *Safari Adventure*. New York: Dutton, 1991.

Latham, Aaron. *The Frozen Leopard*. New York: Prentice-Hall, 1991.

Lourie, Peter. *Amazon: A Young Reader's Look at a Last Frontier*. Honesdale, PA: Caroline House/St. Martin's Press, 1991.

Margolies, Barbara. *Rehewa's Journey: A Visit to Tanzania*. New York: Scholastic, 1990.

Parfit, Michael. *South Light: A Journey to the Last Continent*. New York: Macmillan, 1985.

Preston, Douglas J. *Cities of Gold: A Journey Across the American Southwest in Coronado's Footsteps*. New York: Simon and Schuster, 1992.

Thorndike, Joseph Jacobs. *The Coast: A Journey Down the Atlantic Shore from Maine to Florida*. New York: St. Martin's Press, 1993.

Thurbron, Colin. *Behind the Wall: A Journey Through China*. New York: Atlantic Monthly Press, 1988.

Voices from Around the World. Austin, TX: Steck-Vaughn, 1991.

Wild Ice: Antarctic Journeys. Washington, DC: Smithsonian Institution Press, 1990.

Series

Travel guide series provide much in the way of descriptive writing. The following are examples of publishers' series. Information about travel guides is often included in *Publishers Weekly*. Each series includes handbooks for a number of countries, regions, and cities.

American Automobile Association Tour Books. Heathrow, FL: AAA. Annual.

Baedecker's Guides. New York: Prentice-Hall. Annual.

Blue Guides. New York: Norton. Annual.

Fodor's Travel Guides. New York: Fodor's Travel Publications. Annual.

Frommer's Comprehensive Travel Guides. New York: Prentice-Hall. Annual.

Let's Go Guides. New York: St. Martin's Press. Annual.

Michelin Tourist Guides. New York: Michelin. Annual.

Mobile Travel Guides. New York: Prentice-Hall. Annual.
Stephen Birnbaum Travel Guides. New York: HarperCollins. Annual.

Professional Sources

The use of slides with audio accompaniment is an older audiovisual technique. Many schools have abandoned the medium. It can, however, be very effective for helping students understand visual sequence and how the words and text must be synchronized for the message they wish to deliver to be understood. The sources listed below provide the teacher and library media specialist with some of the more recent articles about how to prepare slide/tape presentations. Several of the sources provide specific instructions in how the method might be used in motivating students to use and explore descriptive language through visuals. As the computer becomes integrated into instruction, it is likely that computerized slide/tape programs will become more widely available.

Bishop, Ann. *Slides, Planning and Producing Slide Programs.* Rochester, NY: Eastman Kodak, 1986.

Bullough, Robert V. *Multi-Image Media.* Englewood Cliffs, NJ: Educational Technology Publications, 1981.

Dennis, Lisl. *Travel Photography: Developing a Personal Style.* New York: Van Nostrand, 1983.

Effective Visual Presentations. Rochester, NY: Eastman Kodak, 1979.

Elberfeld, John K. "Preparing Slide Presentations on Computers." *Computing Teacher* 10, no. 2 (October 1982), pp. 34-35.

Francombe, Anthony. "The Production of Slide/Tape Sequences." *Educational Media International* 2 (June 1974), pp. 24-31.

Frith, Geog H., and Freddy Reynolds. "Slide Tape Shows: A Creative Activity for Gifted Students." *Teaching Exceptional Children* 15, no. 3 (Spring 1983), pp. 151-53.

Heinich, Robert, Michael Molenda, and James D. Russell. *Instructional Media and the New Technologies of Instruction.* New York: Macmillan, 1993.

Hitchens, Howard, ed. 1980 *Producing Slide and Tape Presentations: Readings from 'Audiovisual Instruction' 4.* Washington, DC: Association for Educational Communications and Technology. ED 219060.

Jobe, Holly. *Planning and Producing Slide/Tape Shows.* Scranton, PA: Northeastern Educational Intermediate Unit. Pennsylvania Department of Education, 1978. ED 171319.

Kenny, Michael F., and Raymond F. Schmitt. *Images, Images: The Book of Programmed Multi-Image Production.* Rochester, NY: Eastman Kodak, 1981.

Kert, Isabel. "Creating a Slide-Tape Show." *TESL Talk* 11, no. 2 (Spring 1980), pp. 14-15.

"Planning and Producing a Travelogue." *School Library Media Activities Monthly* 5, no. 10 (June 1989), pp. 36-38.

Rowatt, Robert H. *Slide Tape: A Guide to the Production of Slide-Tape Programmes*. Glasgow, Scotland: Scottish Council for Educational Technology, 1980. ED 211110.

Ryan, Mack. "Preparing a Slide-Tape Program: A Step-by-Step Approach." *Audiovisual Instruction* 20, no. 7 (September 1975), pp. 36-38, 43.

————. "Preparing a Slide-Tape Program: A Step-by-Step Approach (Part II)." *Audiovisual Instruction* 20, no. 9 (November 1975), pp. 36-39.

Schwenk, Jorg. "The Production of a Slide/Tape Sequence." *Educational Media International* 2 (June 1974), pp. 3-6.

Slawson, Ron. *Multi-Image Slide/Tape Programs*. Englewood, CO: Libraries Unlimited, 1988.

Taborn, Stretton. "Making Slide-Tape Programs for the English Classroom." *Classroom English* 15, no. 1 (1980), pp. 14-17.

Thomas, James L. *Nonprint Production for Students, Teachers, and Media Specialists: A Step-by-Step Guide*. Englewood, CO: Libraries Unlimited, 1988.

Tilden, Scott W. "Design Your Organization's Own Slide-Tape Show." *Journal of Educational Communication* 1, no. 2 (September-October 1975), pp. 26-34.

Townsend, Ian. "Producing a Tape-Slide Package: The Final Stages." *Visual Education* (April 1976), pp. 23-24.

————. "Producing a Tape-Slide Package: The Initial Analysis." *Visual Education* (February 1976), pp. 17-19.

————. "Producing a Tape-Slide Package: The Visual Component." *Visual Education* (March 1976), pp. 23-27.

Townsend, John, and John Parker. *A Guide to Producing Tape-Slide Packages, Worksheets, Ancillary Reading*. Sheffield, England: NHS Learning Resources Unit, 1980. ED 222177.

Index